FOUNDATIONS OF MODERN ECONOMICS SERIES

ROBERT DORFMAN *Harvard University*

Prices
and Markets

PRENTICE-HALL, INC. *Englewood Cliffs, New Jersey*

PRENTICE-HALL FOUNDATIONS
OF MODERN ECONOMICS SERIES

Otto Eckstein, *Editor*

Current printing (last digit):
10 9 8 7 6 5 4 3 2

PRENTICE-HALL INTERNATIONAL INC., *London*
PRENTICE-HALL OF AUSTRALIA, PTY., LTD., *Sydney*
PRENTICE-HALL OF CANADA, LTD., *Toronto*
PRENTICE-HALL OF INDIA PVT. LTD., *New Delhi*
PRENTICE-HALL OF JAPAN, INC., *Tokyo*

C

Foundations

of Modern Economics Series

Economics has grown so rapidly in recent years, it has increased so much in scope and depth, and the new dominance of the empirical approach has so transformed its character, that no one book can do it justice today. To fill this need, the Foundations of Modern Economics Series was conceived. The Series, brief books written by leading specialists, reflects the structure, content, and key scientific and policy issues of each field. Used in combination, the Series provides the material for the basic one-year college course. The analytical core of economics is presented in *Prices and Markets* and *National Income Analysis,* which are basic to the various fields of application. *Prices and Markets,* a new book prepared especially for this edition of the Series, takes the beginning student through the elements of that subject step-by-step. *The Price System* is a more sophisticated alternative carried over from the first edition. Two books in the Series, *The Evolution of Modern Economics* and *Economic Development: Past and Present,* can be read without prerequisite and can serve as an introduction to the subject.

The Foundations approach enables an instructor to devise his own course curriculum rather than to follow the format of the traditional textbook. Once analytical principles have been mastered, many sequences of topics can be arranged and specific areas can be explored at length. An instructor not interested in a complete survey course can omit some books and concentrate on a detailed study of a few fields. One-semester courses stressing either macro-

or micro-economics can be readily devised. The instructors guide to the Series indicates the variety of ways the books in the Series can be used.

This Series is an experiment in teaching. The positive response to the first edition has encouraged us to continue, and to develop and improve, the approach. The thoughtful reactions of many teachers who have used the books in the past have been of immense help in preparing the second edition —in improving the integration of the Series, in smoothing some rough spots in exposition, and in suggesting additional topics for coverage.

The books do not offer settled conclusions. They introduce the central problems of each field and indicate how economic analysis enables the reader to think more intelligently about them, to make him a more thoughtful citizen, and to encourage him to pursue the subject further.

Otto Eckstein, *Editor*

Contents

vii

The Task of Economics

CHAPTER ONE

WHAT TO EXPECT

Economics deals with familiar things in what we shall soon recognize as an unfamiliar way. Its topics include buying and selling, borrowing and lending, spending and investing, working and being unemployed, stocks and bonds, and foreign exchange. Its concerns can be as romantic as negotiating oil concessions in the Sahara, or as crass as haggling over the price of a second-hand car. It deals with important events, such as a nation's decision to change the international value of its currency, and unimportant ones, such as a housewife's choice between butter and oleo-margarine. Its range extends from the everyday transactions that we all conduct, to the intricate operations understood by only a handful of government-bond dealers.

What is it that binds all these diverse events together—that makes them part of a single field of study? Basically, they all have two characteristics in common: (1) they involve decisions, and (2) in every case the decisions influence either the way in which the work of the world is organized, or the manner in which the results of that work are used. Any decision about what is to be made and when, and where, and how, and by whom, or about what is to be consumed, and when, and where, and by whom, falls within the purview of economics.

These decisions can be studied from many points of view. Psychologists, sociologists, historians, anthropologists, and other scholars also study decisions, including the kinds of decisions that interest economists, but they examine them from different angles and by different techniques. Typically in all these other disciplines,

1

attention is focused on the factors that *determine* the decision; in economics we are interested primarily in its *consequences*.

Psychologists, for example, concentrate on trying to explain decisions in terms of the built-in tendencies of the human (or animal) mind and the unique experiences of the individual who makes the decisions. Sociologists are especially concerned with the impact on decisions of an individual's status and social position, and what kinds of decisions a particular social structure encourages. Economists, however (though most assuredly interested in pertinent findings culled from all related disciplines), attend to the cumulative *effects* of economic decisions and their interconnections.

Take saving as an example. A psychologist could perhaps demonstrate its relationship to anal eroticism; a historian might trace the connection between patterns of saving behavior and the emergence of the Puritan ethic; a sociologist would probably study the dissimilar attitudes of the various social classes toward saving. The economist treats saving differently. Not overly concerned with causes or connections—such matters as why people save and how the amount they save is affected by their income and social status—he pushes on to study consequences: the effect of saving on other economic decisions (e.g., the decision to lend or invest money); the effect of other economic decisions (e.g., those that influence incomes) on the decision to save. The economist will almost never be interested in your personal decision to save, but he will be very much concerned indeed with the over-all upshot of the saving decisions of you and all the other savers taken together.

ECONOMICS AND PRACTICAL AFFAIRS

The kinds of decisions that concern economists (decisions about what to produce and how, and what to consume and how much) and the point of view taken toward them (the emphasis on the interrelationships among typical decisions and on their consequences in the aggregate) are obviously of great practical importance. Indeed, economics was originally called "political economy" because it dealt almost exclusively with offering advice to governments on matters of national economic policy. But it was quickly discovered that if this advice was to be well-founded it would have to be based on careful study of how policy measures influence people's economic decisions, and of how one set of economic decisions influences others. So it was that the discipline of economics emerged partly to meet the need for a rational basis for national economic policies, and partly in response to a growing interest in economic behavior as significant for scholarly study.

Let us illustrate the kinds of complications that have to be considered in connection with formulating economic policies by picturing a country in which high food prices are causing hardships to wage-earners and their families. To permit or encourage wages to rise could touch off an inflation, and might not help the wage-earners much if the higher wages lead to higher prices for manufactured goods, and the higher prices of manufactures forced farmers to raise their prices still higher. At the same time, measures designed to hold down food prices probably would discourage farmers from increasing production, and so perpetuate the food shortage that lies behind the high food prices. The best policy in this case might well be the paradoxical one of holding the line firmly on wages and manufactured goods prices. The logic behind this policy is that high prices for food products, combined with more moderate prices for the things farmers buy, make food production profitable and thereby stimulate the greater farm production needed to cure the situation.

Such problems as the one we have illustrated are never simple, and the obvious solutions are not always the right ones. A systematic method of analysis, as well as an imposing accumulation of facts about economic decisions, is needed to arrive at sound answers to questions of economic policy.

SOME ASPECTS OF OUR ECONOMIC SYSTEM

Like the atmosphere, our economic system is both ubiquitous and—for the most part, at least—invisible. To be sure, the money in our pockets is visible enough, especially when it changes hands. And we are perfectly well aware of the dozens of economic transactions we make each day—of the paychecks we earn and the purchases we make. But we are generally not aware of most of the many invisible consequences of our transactions, or of the network of interrelations that binds these transactions into a system, the economic system.

For example, when we purchase something—even some insignificant, inexpensive item—we rarely bother to realize that we thereby reduce the dealer's stock of that item. Our purchase, and a few others, reduce his inventory to the point where he places a reorder with his supplier. This reorder, and a few others, induces the supplier to issue a "job order" that causes some of that commodity to be manufactured, mined, imported, or otherwise called into being. These productive activities, in turn, draw down inventories of raw materials, perhaps to the point of inducing reorders of them. They may even cause the manufacturer to increase his workforce or to borrow some money. If he hires someone who was previously unemployed, that new worker will be in a position to increase his rate of purchases. Or if the manufacturer, in his indirect response to our purchase among others, hires a worker away from another industry, he will reduce the workforce available to that industry, and that reduction alone will entail a variety of consequences. If he takes out a loan to finance the new production, he thereby reduces the amount of funds available to other firms, and helps support the rate of interest. But we shall stop here, because it is unnecessary (not to mention practically impossible) to list all the ramifications of our purchase; clearly, the point is that every purchase, in addition to its obvious effect of meeting some need, forms part of the vast signaling system that directs and controls the activity of the economy. And everyone who works in a firm or otherwise contributes resources to the work of the economy not only contributes direct productive effort; he also signals that resources of the type he offers are available at the price he accepts.

Economics studies this signaling system. It deals with the causes, the consequences, the ramifications of economic transactions. It studies the effects of transactions as they spread throughout the economy, helping both to induce still other transactions and to inhibit some that might have occurred. In the light of this analysis, it evaluates how well a particular economic system meets the social needs it is supposed to satisfy. It compares the performance of different possible systems of economic organization. It formulates the requirements for good performance and suggests changes that will improve the operation of the system. And it does this in a

3

sophisticated way that keeps in view not only the direct, obvious effects of any transaction, but its indirect, hidden, possibly more important ramifications.

Consider, for example, minimum-wage laws. Their intended effect is to improve the operation of the economy by increasing the incomes of very low-paid workers. That would be their result, too, but for the indirect effects—one of which is to increase the costs of operation in the industries that have been paying less than minimum wages. These higher costs may be reflected in higher prices for the products, reduced purchases of them, and, in the end, less employment and lower incomes for some of the very people the law was intended to help. Another indirect effect of compelling higher wages may be to induce employers to try to produce the same output with fewer workers, either by increasing the efficiency of their operations or by raising the level of mechanization and automation in their plants. This response, too, will reduce employment in the low-wage, low-skill industries. This is not to say that minimum-wage legislation is futile, though some economists have drawn that conclusion. It is to say that its desirability cannot be established merely on the grounds of good intentions and beneficial first consequences. One must consider the whole story of how the economic system responds to such a change.

Our economic system is largely automatic but its operation is not, like the stars in their courses, preordained and beyond the scope of human influence. On the contrary, the economic system is a social instrument that we can modify as we please. We are constantly changing it, in both major respects and minor ones, and have always been doing so. We are enacting and changing tariffs and taxes, antitrust laws and farm support programs, fair-trade acts, child-labor laws, highway improvements, urban zoning ordinances, irrigation and hydroelectric developments, usury laws, and food-and-drug regulations. All these and many other measures are consciously designed to change the economy so that it operates more to our liking, and such effort to control and improve the working of the economy is one of the main concerns of governments everywhere and always. But all such measures bring some number of unintended, indirect consequences along with their intended, direct ones. The task of economics is to disclose these indirect effects so that proposed changes and policies can be evaluated in the light of all their consequences. More than that: since we live in an economy, we should understand its operations so that we can react intelligently to the results it produces, both desirable and undesirable. We can improve what we can, and should accept what we must, only in the light of such understanding. Economics studies the economy from this point of view.

THE PROBLEM OF ALLOCATION

The description of an economic system and its operations is too large a task for this small book, and even for a single course—and thus a realistic first course in economics necessarily takes a broad view of the whole field without probing deeply into any one aspect. This part of your initial course deals with one of the most fundamental aspects, on which many of the other parts depend, called "the problem of allocation." We shall describe the genesis of this problem.

The origins of the human race and of the economies it has created are hidden in the dim past. Paleolithic men lived in small tribes, in caves and forests. Even the most primitive agriculture was unknown to them: they hunted, fished, and scrounged for plants. The distinction we are accustomed to make between the civilized world of mankind and the wild sphere of nature was hardly applicable; man was simply an omnivorous animal sharing a wild domain with the other omnivores, carnivores, and herbivores—he had not yet undertaken to control his environment.

Perhaps 10,000 years ago agriculture first appeared. This was a fundamental turning-point in human affairs, very likely the most fundamental in all history. Then the line was first drawn between the world that simply grew and the world that man controlled. We can only conjecture the social revolution that this entailed. For the first time the members of the tribe had to respect, and to contest, each other's property rights. A whole new set of customs, taboos, and practices had to be invented to make it practical to cultivate fields and tend domestic animals. Communities, with all their rights, obligations, and proscriptions, existed before then, but nothing in the social fabric had to take account of any economic effort more complicated than organizing a hunting party. The real Garden of Eden was a thorny garden; with the invention of agriculture man departed from it forever.

As the hunting tribe was replaced by the agricultural community, the social structure became much more complicated. With stable villages and land to be protected, professional warrior castes, ruling classes, and organized priesthoods emerged. Villages were welded into countries. The first rigid social differentiation among men arose—based, it should be noted, on a differentiation of political rather than economic tasks. But more was to follow. The new wealth (comparatively speaking) and stability freed energies for undertakings more varied than food production: more elaborate clothing, improved implements, more advanced kinds of pottery and other household goods came into use—and better weapons for the warriors, and luxury goods for the rulers and priests.

It was also discovered very, very early that many of the required tasks could be performed more efficiently by specially trained and talented people who devoted full time to them, than by the jack-of-all-trades farmers and herders. A small number of artisans became differentiated from the agricultural majority, and with this there arose the practices of division of labor and domestic trade.[1] Thus began, also, the closely knit interdependence of economic effort that has increasingly characterized the work of the world ever since. If agriculture was the fundamental discovery, the division of labor was its most important corollary.

But the division of labor, although inconceivably more productive than the same work done on an individual basis, brings problems in its train. Among other things, it requires vastly more coordination. Where there is division of labor, each man depends for his necessities on others who may be utter strangers to him, and far remote. He, in turn, is working to supply the needs of men he does not know. How can a man know what utter strangers will want from him? How can he be confident that someone, somewhere, will provide what he needs?

It is little wonder that the evolution of self-sufficient farm communities into modern, integrated economies is a very gradual process despite its manifest advantages. (Here we have shifted abruptly to the present tense because we are still

---

[1] Of course, the bees and other social insects had developed division of labor eons previously. International trade, of a sort, probably antedated domestic trade, as when tribes whose territories included salt deposits traded in some fashion with tribes that possessed other localized resources.

in the midst of that stage of economic development.) One of the great problems in India and Pakistan (for example) is to persuade farmers to grow crops for the market rather than for their own consumption. Their farms would be vastly more productive if they did so, but the farmers are justifiably wary of becoming dependent on the operations of an economy that still has to prove that *it* can meet *their* needs with adequate reliability. The bulk of the human race still fends for itself when it comes to the prime necessities of life.

It is not surprising, therefore, that the step from the agricultural community to the integrated economy has occupied the whole of recorded history and is still only half accomplished. It is not surprising, even, that in such an ancient civilization as the Chinese the step was never taken until imposed from the outside. There is more cause to be surprised that in Western Europe, in the late Middle Ages, somehow a great change began. Towns began to grow up around the courts of barons and bishops, and the occasional village artisans congregated there into guilds. Eventually, caravans of goods began to travel the roads from town to fair to town. Trade finally reached the point where all were dependent on it in one way or another—and it was at that point (the exact date, even the century, is still in dispute) that capitalism as we know it emerged.

Our impressionistic sketch of economic history should convey several morals. It should remind us in the first place that our economic system is neither a perfect, immutable, eternal thing, nor a heritage too sacred to be tampered with. Instead it is a stage in a slow evolution, constantly deflected by historical accident, in which social institutions are tried, often abandoned, modified by slow and tentative accretions—all in the effort to enjoy the advantages of the division of labor and yet have our needs reliably met. Its slow and painful growth is a measure of the difficulty of the task.

Finally, this sketch should bring out that although division of labor is an essential feature of a productive economy, it entails a difficult social problem: that of coordinating effort (or, synonymously, of allocating resources to different tasks). This problem has been solved in different ways in different times and places—each solution, remember, being the result of slow, tentative social evolution.

In feudal Europe, for example, the problem was solved by the manorial system. Each manor was practically an independent economic unit, and immemorial custom prescribed each man's job, and even the methods he was to use. This system of economic coordination by status and custom is perhaps the most ancient and widespread of all; the caste system in contemporary India is a vestige of its use there. The prime defect of that method is its excessive rigidity: it adapts to changing world conditions with glacial sluggishness and it stubbornly resists internal innovation.

In the U.S.S.R., economic coordination is achieved by centralized direction. Russia's is probably the only instance in all history where the main lines of effort in an extensive and elaborate economy have been determined by central authority— an undertaking which could hardly have been conceived before the development of modern techniques of communication and bureaucratic organization. The success of the Soviet experiment remains to be seen. Thus far it has scored some remarkable achievements and has been the victim of some equally remarkable blunders. This book will explore some of the forbidding difficulties that confront any version of centralized economic planning.

The most successful method of economic coordination thus far in history is reliance on a free market economy. This method is so subtle and intricate that it could not have been invented; it had to simply happen, as it did. For this same reason it is hard to understand—but we shall try to present it in a way that will not invite misunderstanding.

THE FREE MARKET ECONOMY

In spite of its intricacy, the basic idea of a free market economy is very simple. It is the idea of decentralizing control of the economy down to units of manageable proportions, coupled with a stupendously efficient method for conveying information among the decentralized units, and a highly effective method of motivating the units to perform their appropriate tasks efficiently.

The method of information transmittal is the price system. The great social discovery embodied in it is the almost incredible fact that practically all an economic unit has to know about the world outside itself in order to do its work well is the prices of the things it buys and sells—provided that these prices are properly determined. The unit doesn't have to know who wants its products or even how much they want, but only how much they are willing to pay. It doesn't have to know who has the things it needs or how much of them is available in the world, but only how much it has to pay for them. Who would have thought, *a priori,* that an economy could run efficiently on that scanty basis? Who would have thought that this was all firms had to know in order to produce the right amounts of all the things that consumers and other firms need? But so it is.[2] On top of that, no one has to decide on the prices; left to themselves they provide the correct information— another well-nigh incredible fact! The intricacy of the system lies in how automatically-adjusting prices convey just the right information to economic units.

The motivating aspect of the free market system is less subtle and, there is reason to believe, less efficient. In fact, the system often leads to socially undesirable behavior (e.g., production of shoddy products) and sometimes provides inadequate incentives for desirable behavior. This is the profit system, the idea of rewarding economic units in proportion to their profitability. In one crucial respect it is administratively sound: it assigns rewards and penalties to each decision-maker largely in proportion to the quality of his own performance, and to each worker in proportion to the value of his contribution to the work of the economy. That is, it makes each man bear responsibility for his own decisions and actions. But it does so only in intent and in principle. In practice, under the profit system, men frequently benefit from other men's achievements and suffer for other men's mistakes; there is a large element of luck and lottery. Besides, even when rewards and penalties are correctly assigned (from the administrative viewpoint) they are often of disproportionate magnitude.

These are serious defects, and the purpose of most contemporary modifications of the system (e.g., social welfare legislation, progressive income taxation, increased government control over the level of national income) is to mitigate them. As we

---

[2] That appropriately chosen prices can convey all the information necessary for an efficiently working economy is a mathematical theorem which, naturally, was discovered after economies had been working on this principle for many generations.

noted at the outset, it isn't always easy to correct one defect without creating a worse one. The system, we insist again, is still evolving.

A FRAMEWORK FOR ANALYSIS

One of the main purposes of theorizing, especially in the social sciences, is to make us self-conscious and explicit about our reasoning. This has several advantages. It forces us to be aware of the assumptions that we use so that we are alert to the circumstances under which our conclusions are and are not valid. By the same token it prevents us from changing our assumptions and concepts unconsciously in the course of an argument—a common source of muddy reasoning. When two people come to conflicting conclusions it is generally because they have argued from different premises. If their premises have been made explicit, the source of their disagreement can be detected and discussed intelligently. Of course all the careful formality and theorizing in the world cannot provide sure protection against indulging in unnoticed assumptions, but it helps.

The purpose of this book is to make us aware of the grounds of our beliefs about what determines prices and how prices influence the economy. We are not going to find many surprises, because economic theorizing rarely unearths unexpected phenomena of importance. But it does deepen our understanding of recognized relationships and provides a coherent framework for discussing economic issues and policies.

It is amazing how many complicated assumptions we invoke whenever we think about economic matters. Our brief discussion of minimum-wage laws (a few pages back) is a prime example. It would be instructive to try to list all the relevant assumptions that were taken for granted in those few sentences. We said that businessmen would be likely to increase their prices after the minimum-wage laws were in effect. Why would they raise prices then if they had not done so before? We said that the higher prices would reduce their sales. Why? And would not the reduction in sales lead to a canceling reduction in the prices? Our reasoning was correct enough, but its grounds were certainly obscure.

Some of the general principles implicit in our discussion of minimum wages are used repeatedly in economic reasoning, and these should be made explicit at the outset. One is the notion of underlying forces or tendencies that operate independently. We cannot be sure that a minimum-wage law will be followed by higher prices for the products most affected, because some events might occur simultaneously that tend to depress the prices. We therefore have to reason about the probable effects of any change by assuming that no other relevant changes occur before the effects of the first change become evident.

Indeed, the responses of an economic system to changes in conditions take time; although a minimum-wage law tends to reduce employment in the industries most affected, this does not happen overnight. But we are not interested generally in the state of affairs the day after a minimum-wage law has been enacted—we judge its effects rather by the state of affairs that it tends to produce after *all* the significant reactions have taken place. All this was implicit in our informal discussion.

To make this point of view explicit, we now establish the ground rule that whenever we consider an economic change we shall assume that no other relevant changes occur except those that are consequences of the initiating change. Furthermore, we shall concentrate on positions of "equilibrium," which, roughly speaking, are states of the economy in which everyone has adjusted to the current situation as well as he can. Here is a more formal and exact definition of equilibrium:

An economy is in equilibrium when every firm and household in it can carry out the decisions that seem most advantageous to it in the current circumstances.[3]

The essential force of this definition is suggested by an illustration. Every shoe manufacturer decides how many shoes he wishes to manufacture and how many to hold in inventory, in the light of the current price of shoes, price of leather, and other data. Independently of these decisions, every consumer decides on how many shoes he wishes to purchase, taking into consideration the price of shoes, his own income, and other data. No matter what these decisions may be, it is arithmetically certain that in the end: Number of Shoes Manufactured = Number of Shoes Purchased + Change in Inventories.

This equation is a truism which will apply no matter what the manufacturers and consumers decide, and whether or not the economy is in equilibrium. But if the number of shoes that consumers decide to purchase is different from the number that the manufacturers had expected (say, more), then the manufacturers will find their inventories smaller than they had planned and desired. The manufacturers will not be able to carry out their aims (decision with respect to inventories), and the economy will not be in equilibrium. Since the manufacturers thus find their decision to be infeasible, they will change it either by increasing their output, or by raising prices to reduce purchases, or in some other way. In one way or another, at any rate, they will always try to move toward equilibrium.

The most useful method of practical economic analysis rests upon this concept of an equilibrium and upon the belief that the equilibrating forces in an economy are so strong that actual conditions in an economy will not remain far from the equilibrium conditions for very long. This latter factor makes it possible to predict the consequences of any change in circumstances by determining the equilibrium conditions of the economy under the new circumstances, and predicting that the economy will move toward the new equilibrium.

The equilibrium method was implicit in our discussion of minimum-wage laws, the initial effect of which, as we saw, is to increase costs of production in the industries that are paying less than the proposed minimum. We also saw that this increase is likely to cause producers in those industries to change their decisions about the quantities of both the unskilled labor they wish to employ, and the goods they wish to produce. Since such a law does not alter consumers' purchasing decisions, however, a disequilibrium has been created. The disequilibrium may be resolved in the way previously cited: by an increase in prices and a decrease in production, the combination of which is certain to lower the demand.

This general (equilibrium) method is known as the method of *comparative statics*. It is comparative because it compares equilibria in two different circumstances; it is static because it passes over the process of readjustment, which may be painful and prolonged, and concentrates on the quiescent conditions appropriate

[3] Paraphrased from J. R. Hicks, *Capital and Growth* (New York: Oxford University Press, 1965), p. 15.

to the old and the new equilibria. By the use of comparative statics we can appraise economic policies—at least partially—simply by studying their effects on economic equilibrium. This is fortunate, because the study of equilibrium is far and away the easiest kind of economic analysis. Apart from a few digressions, we shall remain within its confines throughout this book.

THE STRUCTURE OF THIS BOOK

Until we reach the final chapters we shall be concerned with the forces that determine the price of a single commodity, and the amount of it produced and consumed. This is the fundamental building-block of the *theory of economic allocation*. In the next chapter we shall see how producers of a commodity, and consumers of it, interact to determine a price at which the amounts that the producers wish to make and the consumers wish to purchase are equal—an equilibrium price as we have defined it.

This discussion of market forces, however, will not bring out all the relationships of the prices and quantities so determined to producers' costs on the one hand or to consumers' wants on the other. The following three chapters look into these matters. Chapter 3 is devoted to the relationship between the quantity of a commodity produced and its production costs. Chapter 4 considers producers' efforts to keep costs down, and their implications for the level of wages and the prices of raw materials used in production. Chapter 5 analyzes consumers' decisions, and particularly the relationship between consumers' wants and the quantities of different commodities they buy at different prices.

This group of chapters devoted to price and quantity determination is based on a simplifying assumption about producers—namely, that no producer perceives that he can influence the prices of the things that he buys and sells. This assumption is frequently justifiable, more frequently than superficial appearances might lead you to believe. For example, a producer of ball-point pens "suggests" the price at which his pens ought to be sold. But he has no choice in practice except to suggest the price being charged by other manufacturers of comparable products. On the other hand, this assumption is not always applicable, and in fact Chapter 6 is devoted to two important types of situation in which it is not.

Finally, the explanation of a single price and the quantity produced of a single commodity is not of much importance. That explanation is significant only as the solution to a problem of allocating resources, and no allocation problem exists unless there are at least two commodities among which economic efforts and resources are to be divided. Our real goal, then, is to understand how the markets for different commodities interact to guide the economic efforts of an entire community. This is the subject of Chapters 7 and 8; all else is actually prologue.

Supply and Demand

CHAPTER TWO

Whenever anything worthy of public concern happens to an economy, people tend to furrow their brow knowingly and explain the phenomenon away with the pat phrase, "It's caused by the forces of supply and demand." They are usually right (although most of them can't explain why). Supply and demand most assuredly *are* at the bottom of practically everything that happens in an economy: they determine the quantity of every commodity that is produced, the amount purchased, and the price it commands. But (unfortunately, perhaps) even this time-honored cliché really won't explain any economic incident very fully, because "supply" and "demand," like many other terms, are empty words until we have defined them carefully and have seen how the activities they represent interact. Our present task, therefore—and no task is more important to an understanding of how an economy works— is to do just this.

The most important economic facts about a commodity are the quantity of it produced and the price it commands. These are determined simultaneously (and at this point, not surprisingly, we hope) by the forces of supply and demand. To see how these forces operate, we have to do what may seem a strange thing: turn the relationship around and ask how prices influence the amounts of a commodity that are supplied and demanded. An example will help show why this is necessary, and will also give concrete form to the economic forces we are studying.

Bituminous coal will provide our example. Coal is gathered from more than 7,000 working (productive) mines—underground mines, strip mines, a few auger mines.[1] The ages of these mines

[1] In an auger mine the ore is extracted by a revolving bit (an auger) that looks like an enormous screw.

range from those being opened from time to time today, to those that are remarkably ancient; and of course some tap thick veins of coal while others tap thin ones, and some are deep and difficult to work, whereas others are shallow and convenient. Costs of operation vary widely in this industry, as in most others. The result is that whatever the price of goal may be, there will be some mines and parts of mines that can be operated profitably (in the sense that the price will exceed the costs of operation) and some that cannot be. Coal mine operators keep a watchful eye on price trends; they extract coal from the profitable mines and close down the others. Thus the higher the price of coal, the more mines it pays to operate, and the larger the volume of coal that is produced.

These facts can be summarized and made specific by a kind of table called a *supply schedule.*

A supply schedule is a table that shows the amount of a commodity that will be produced per year in response to every possible price.

Table 2-1 SUPPLY SCHEDULE FOR BITUMINOUS COAL
(Hypothetical data)

Price ($ per ton)	Volume of Production (Million of tons per year)
6.00	485
5.75	475
5.50	462
5.25	450
5.00	438
4.75	422
4.50	400
4.25	378
4.00	350
.	.
.	.

Table 2-1 is an example of a supply schedule. According to this table, if the price of coal is $4.50 a ton at the minehead, it will pay to operate mines capable of producing 400 million tons a year. That was essentially the situation in the early 1960's. If the price of coal were to rise to $5 a ton, it would pay to open up additional mines capable of producing 38 million tons a year, for a total of 438 million tons. On the other hand, if the price were to fall to $4.25 a ton, some mines that operated at $4.50 a ton would become unprofitable, and output would fall by 22 million tons. Such a table, in short, summarizes the responses of an industry to changes in the price of its product. A good many considerations lie behind such a curve, and we shall consider them in the next chapters. But for the purposes of price determination, the most significant data about an industry are contained in its supply schedule.

The same facts can be displayed more vividly by a graph known as a *supply curve.*

A supply curve is a graph of a supply schedule, showing the amount of a commodity that will be produced per year in response to every possible price.

The supply curve corresponding to the data in Table 2-1 is shown in Fig. 2-1. In this graph, possible prices of coal are marked along the vertical axis and possible volumes of production along the horizontal axis. Each price-quantity pair listed in the supply schedule is plotted on the graph. For example, the dashed lines indicate that a price of $4.50 will elicit a supply of 400 million tons a year. The gaps remaining on the graph when the data in the supply schedule have been plotted are then filled in by a smooth curve.

The supply curve vividly presents some features of the supply schedule that are not easily seen in a table. In this case, for example, the supply makes it clear that when high volumes of output are reached, it becomes increasingly expensive to increase production still further. This is shown by the increasing steepness of the curve, so that larger and larger increases in price are required to induce successive increments of, say, 10 million tons after output has reached about 450 million. At this production level some very poor mines must be brought into the picture and each successive increase in output requires resort to significantly poorer ones. According to the graph, outputs of above 500 million tons a year are almost prohibitively expensive to obtain.[2]

The supply curve drawn for the coal industry is typical of those pertaining to many industries. In agriculture and manufacturing, as well as in mining, costs of production are different in different establishments. Even within a single factory or farm, after an efficient level of output has been attained, increases in production can be coaxed out only by resorting to poorer land, older machines, overtime work, and the like, all of which increase costs of operation. An industry will not increase its output from any going level unless the price rises enough to make the more costly production worthwhile. Conversely, if the price falls, the plants and parts of plants that are most expensive to operate will go out of production, and output will fall. This behavior will generate a supply curve similar to the one we have drawn for coal.

[2] Warning: these are hypothetical data. In fact, 630 million tons were mined in 1947, the industry's peak year.

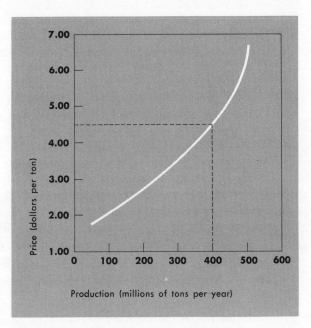

FIG. 2-1 A typical supply curve. Larger amounts are offered at higher prices.

Price (dollars per ton)

Production (millions of tons per year)

THE EFFECT OF PRICE ON DEMAND

You know from your own experience that you are more careful in using things that cost more. Everyone is lavish with water; few are lavish with champagne. This suggests that the effect of price on consumption or demand is just the opposite from what it is on supply: the higher the price of a commodity, the less that will be consumed. This is true, and for a variety of reasons.

Consider coal again. Very little is used nowadays by private households. Electric utilities are the largest consumers, and steel plants are next, followed by a variety of other industries. When the price of coal rises, these different types of users react in ways that differ in detail but lead always to the same result: the reduced use of coal. To get a good idea of the reactions that take place when the price of coal rises, we need look no farther than the most important users, the electric utilities. A power company will meet an increase in coal prices by taking one or more of three different measures. It may operate some "convertible" power plants, stations whose boilers can be switched from coal-burning to oil-burning with little trouble. If so, it will switch them from coal use to oil use when coal becomes expensive and back again when coal becomes more economical. Second, every power company of any size has a variety of stations, some coal-fired, some oil-fired, some gas-fired, some hydroelectric. It will shift its load when fuel prices change, generating a smaller proportion of its power in coal-burning stations when the price of coal increases. Third, power companies are constantly replacing, modernizing, and expanding their plants. They will design the new equipment to use coal or gas or nuclear fuel depending on which fuel they expect to be cheapest—a judgment that is strongly influenced by the current price of coal. When coal prices are high, new equipment is designed to use other fuels, and the coal industry loses customers for a long time in the future. In a variety of ways, then, power companies can and do cut back on the use of coal when its price is high.

But that is not the end of it. An increase in the price of coal raises the generating costs of utilities that use coal and therefore the price of the power they sell. Higher electricity prices naturally influence the decisions made by electric-power users. For example, when a homeowner is deciding whether to buy an electric dryer, a gas dryer, or a new clothes line his decision will be affected by the price of power which, we have seen, reflects the price of coal. There is a chain of influence that extends to the ultimate consumers: higher coal prices mean higher electricity prices, higher electricity prices mean less use of electricity, less use of electricity means less use of coal by coal-burning power companies.

These are just some of the responses of an economy to an increase in the price of coal. The details are unimportant except to call to mind the variety of ways in which an increase in the price of a commodity discourages its use. The response of consumers to a price change may be prompt or slow—in the case of coal it tends to be slow because of the vast amount of equipment that is tied to particular sources of energy—but its direction is universal: the higher the price, the smaller the use.

In strict analogy with what we found when studying supply, the effects of price changes on demand can be expressed in a *demand schedule*.

A demand schedule is a table that shows the amount of a commodity that will be consumed per year at each possible price.

Table 2-2 DEMAND SCHEDULE FOR BITUMINOUS COAL
(Hypothetical data)

Price ($ per ton)	Level of Consumption (Million of tons per year)
6.00	284
5.75	300
5.50	314
5.25	335
5.00	352
4.75	375
4.50	400
4.25	428
4.00	453
3.75	485
3.50	520
.	.
.	.

Table 2-2, a demand schedule for coal, illustrates this concept. According to these data, 400 million tons a year would be consumed at a price of $4.50 a ton. If the price were to rise to $5.00 a ton, consumption would fall to an annual rate of 352 million tons. This decline would not occur overnight; we have already seen that some of the most important responses to a change in the price of coal are slowed down to the pace of power-plant renovation. But if the price of coal rises to a new level, consumption will sag gradually as both coal users and the customers of coal users react, until the new, lower level is reached.

Just as in the case of supply, the data in the demand schedule can be presented

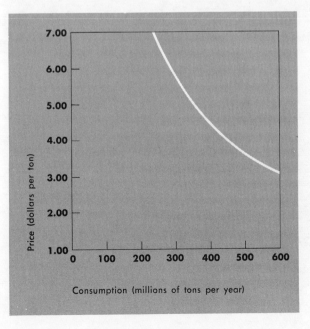

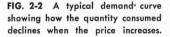

FIG. 2-2 A typical demand curve showing how the quantity consumed declines when the price increases.

Consumption (millions of tons per year)

most vividly in the form of a demand curve. A demand curve is a graph of a demand schedule, showing the amount of a commodity that will be consumed per year at each possible price.

Figure 2-2 displays the data of Table 2-2 in the form of a demand curve. It is interpreted just as the supply curve was.

SUPPLY AND DEMAND IN THE MARKET

The supply and demand schedules contain all the data that determine the price of the commodity and the quantity that will be produced and consumed. They express both the wishes of consumers (how much they are willing to pay for different amounts of the commodity) and the capabilities of producers (how much they can produce profitably at different selling prices). These data are brought together in the market—that is, in the dealings of the people who buy and sell the commodity; the supply and demand schedules show just how this happens. And if we plot the supply and demand curves on a single graph we can easily compare the amounts supplied and demanded at every price. This is done in Fig. 2-3.

Suppose, to begin with, that the price of coal is $5 a ton. The supply curve shows that it will be profitable at that price to operate coal mines with an aggregate capacity of 438 million tons a year, but the demand curve shows that consumers will desire only 352 million tons at that price. With producers offering more coal than consumers are willing to buy, the price will have to give way. The supply schedule shows that producers of 422 million tons can operate profitably at a price of $4.75. Some of these, finding it impossible to sell their coal at $5 a ton, will offer it at a lower price, and the mines that were finding customers will have to follow

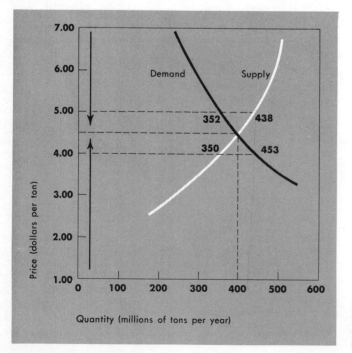

FIG. 2-3 The market diagram. Equilibrium price and quantity are determined by the crossing of the supply and demand curves.

suit. This, indeed, will be true for any producer charging a price above $4.50, the price at which the two curves cross, because supply exceeds demand at those prices. The downward pressure on prices is indicated by the downward-pointing arrow.

The pressures are just the opposite when the price is below the crossing point. At a price of $4 a ton, for example, it will be profitable to produce only 350 million tons a year, although demand will be some 100 million tons a year greater. In this case, dealers' inventories will be drawn down, and some users will find their orders delayed or refused. Many users will be willing to pay more than the going price if necessary to obtain delivery; the demand schedule shows that consumers of 428 million tons are willing to pay $4.25 a ton. The price will therefore tend to rise, and this increase will in turn elicit stepped-up production. All this is suggested by the upward-pointing arrow in the range of prices below $4.50 a ton.

For prices below $4.50 a ton, each small increase in prices narrows the gap between demand and supply by simultaneously snuffing out some demand and calling forth some new supply. As the number of unsatisfied orders diminishes, the upward pressure on the price relaxes, until finally, at the crossing point, demand and supply are in balance. The same is true in the range of prices above the crossing point. Here each decline in the price stimulates some new demand and simultaneously drives out of production some of the barely profitable mines. The pressure of overproduction is gradually reduced until the crossing point is reached. But at the crossing point, all is in balance. Production is neatly meshed with consumption. The mines that can be operated profitably at that price produce just the amount that consumers want to use at that price. There is neither upward nor downward pressure on price. This, accordingly, is called the *equilibrium point;* when it has been attained the market is said to be in equilibrium.

> The equilibrium price of a commodity is the price at which the amounts demanded and supplied are equal. The equilibrium quantity is the level of demand and supply corresponding to that price.

Notice that this equilibrium satisfies the definition we gave in the first chapter. When the price is $4.50 a ton, each consumer can buy the amount that he wishes, and each producer can sell all the coal that he can produce profitably. At no other price is this true.

Since the equilibrium price and quantity are graphically shown by the point at which the supply and demand curves cross, the demand curve-supply curve diagram neatly synopsize the "forces of supply and demand." The conditions of supply and demand determine the shapes and positions of the two curves, and the curves themselves determine whether there will be an upward or downward pressure on prices, or neither, and what the equilibrium price and quantity will be.

CHANGES IN SUPPLY CONDITIONS

The foregoing analysis explained how the equilibrium price of a commodity is determined. The actual price is another matter. Actual prices are always prices in transition, prices moving from yesterday's historical value toward today's equilibrium. If a commodity's supply and demand conditions remained the same for a long period of time, the price would gradually reach the equilibrium value and stay there. But, in point of fact, conditions of supply and demand are constantly changing, and the equilibrium prices and quantities are constantly changing correspondingly. The reactions of prices to such changes are the topic of this and the next section.

By *supply condition* we mean *all circumstances that affect the supply of a commodity except its price*—i.e., all the factors that determine the shape and position of the supply curve. Whenever one or more of these conditions changes, the quantity that will be offered at each price changes, too—that is to say, the supply curve moves to a new position.

Many things can change a supply schedule. For example, the supply curve for a manufactured good changes whenever an invention or other technical development changes its cost of production. But the most significant influences on the position of a supply curve are the prices of the raw materials, the labor, and the other ingredients used in producing the commodity. Whenever the price of steel changes, so do the costs of producing automobiles and many other products. Therefore, the amount of a steel-using product that can be produced profitably at any price changes; that is to say, its supply curve shifts.

As an example, suppose that wage rates in coal mining increase by 50¢ an hour and that miners extract on the average about 2 tons an hour. This wage change then amounts to an increase in production cost of 25¢ a ton. The effect on the supply schedule is easy to see. (See Table 2-3.) At a price of $4.50 a ton, it was profitable to operate mines capable of producing 400 million tons a year before the wage change. After the wage change, each ton costs 25¢ more to extract. Therefore, those very same mines and shafts will be profitable at a price of $4.75 a ton *or more*. On the new supply schedule, therefore, a price of $4.75 a ton will correspond to an output of 400 million tons a year. The reasoning is the same for every other price. After the wage increase, every price of coal will call forth the same production that a price 25¢ lower called forth before the increase. The new supply schedule is recorded, along with the old, in Table 2-3.

Table 2-3   EFFECT OF WAGE INCREASE ON SUPPLY OF COAL
(Hypothetical data)

Price ($ per ton)	Volume of Production (Million tons per year)	
	Before Wage Increase	After Wage Increase
6.00	485	475
5.75	475	462
5.50	462	450
5.25	450	438
5.00	438	422
4.75	422	400
4.50	400	378
4.25	378	350
4.00	350	325
.	.	.
.	.	.

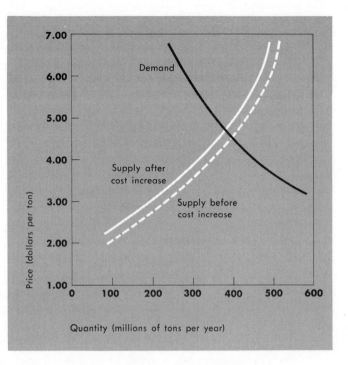

The supply curves derived from the two supply schedules are compared in Fig. 2-4. Graphically, the effect of the increase in production cost of 25¢ a ton has been simply to shift the supply curve rigidly upward by 25¢. As soon as the new costs go into effect, so do the new supply curve and the new equilibrium point, although the adjustments to the new conditions may take some time. The new equilibrium point is northwest of the old one, at a price of $4.60 a ton and an output of 390 million tons a year. But the new equilibrium is not attained presto-chango by magic—it takes time and effort. The industry may respond to the new level of wages in any of a number of different ways (though they all terminate eventually at the same equilibrium position); we shall follow through only one possibility.

Newspaper discussions of a prospective wage increase, or other cost increase, generally assume that increases in costs will be reflected fully in prices. So let us assume that the mine operators try to pass along the entire cost increase. If the industry was in equilibrium at $4.50 a ton before the wage increase, the operators will then raise the price to $4.75 a ton. At this price, according to the new supply schedule, the operators will offer a supply of 400 million tons. But the demand schedule has not changed, and only 375 million tons will be demanded. With production running ahead of demand, some mine operators will find their stocks piling up and will be willing to sell, still profitably, at *less* than $4.75 a ton. The price will sag until, at $4.60 a ton, the quantity demand has risen to 390 million tons a year and the amount supplied has fallen to that same figure (assuming no further changes in the interim). At this price alone the amount producers are willing to supply is equal to the quantity consumers wish to purchase.

The 25¢-a-ton increase in cost thus has a double effect: it diminishes equi- **19** librium output by 10 million tons a year, and it increases equilibrium price by 10¢

a ton. This second effect is especially noteworthy. Producers and consumers have now come to share the burden of the cost increase; the price per ton has risen substantially less than the cost per ton. The mine owners, of course, do not normally intend to share the burden with their customers, but market forces compel it.

The data we have used are special but the qualitative conclusions we have reached are general.

> If the costs of producing a commodity change, its equilibrium price will change in the same direction but by a smaller amount, and its equilibrium quantity will change in the opposite direction.

CHANGES IN DEMAND CONDITIONS

The amount of a commodity demanded by customers depends on many factors other than its price. Among them are current tastes and fashions, the prices of other commodities that can be used for similar purposes, the prices of commodities that use it as a raw material, and the incomes of potential buyers. All these factors contribute to making the demand schedule what it is at any time, and when any of them change, it changes. Thus, demand curves can shift just as supply curves can, and the analysis of the effect of such a shift on the equilibrium of a commodity is parallel.

For example, the amount of coal demanded at every price will fall if the price of a competing fuel, such as natural gas, is reduced. The effect of such a change is shown in Fig. 2-5. The similarity of this diagram to Fig. 2-4 is obvious, and the analysis follows exactly the lines already familiar. From it we conclude:

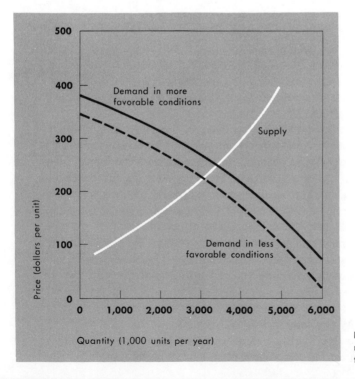

Quantity (1,000 units per year)

FIG. 2-5 Effect of increase in demand. Equilibrium price and quantity both increase.

A decrease in the amount of a commodity demanded at every price (called a decrease in demand) can be represented by a downward shift in the demand curve. It results in decreases in both the equilibrium price and the equilibrium level of sales. An increase in demand has the opposite effects.

This conclusion is subject to one important reservation, however. In practice, the most frequent and prevalent cause of shifts in demand curves is changes in consumers' incomes; when consumers' incomes change, their demand curves shift for almost all the commodities they buy. But then, the effect of these changes in income on the equilibrium price and quantity of any single commodity cannot be analyzed by looking simply at the supply and demand curves for that commodity. Too much else is going on. For example, the prices of other commodities (some of them perhaps seemingly unrelated) are changing under the impact of the same cause, and these price changes are likely to affect both the supply and the demand curves of the commodity we are interested in. A far more elaborate and inclusive kind of analysis that we can present here is needed to deal with changes that affect many markets simultaneously.

MARKETS AND THEIR STRUCTURES

Prices do not change by themselves, but only when buyers and sellers decide to change them. The characteristics and relationships of the buyers and sellers of a commodity therefore have an important bearing on the way in which its price is formed and changed.

All the people who buy and sell a commodity in the ordinary course of their affairs, considered as a group, are called the *market* for that commodity. A description of the numbers and relationships among the buyers and sellers is called the *structure of the market*.

By these definitions, a market is a constantly shifting group of people rather than a place or an identifiable social institution. The coal market consists of mine operators, steel mills, electric-power companies, coal dealers, and so on. The wheat market is not merely the Chicago Board of Trade (the "wheat pit"), but the wheat farmers, the elevator operators, the brokers, the millers, the speculators, and the many other people who buy and sell wheat. All these are affected by the price of the commodity they deal in, and by their actions they influence the very same price, as we have already seen.

Markets are diverse in a large number of ways. There are millions of buyers in the retail clothing market, but only a few dozen in the market for Rembrandts or "federal funds" (one-day loans of bank reserves). The stock market is tightly organized and raucous, while the retail diamond market is loosely organized and sedate. But the most important characteristic of a market for the understanding of price formation is the number of sellers in it. From this point of view there are three important types of markets: *competitive markets, monopolies* (from the Greek *mono* = one, and *polien* = to sell), and *oligopolies* (from *oligo* = few, and *polien*).

A market is competitive if buyers and sellers are so numerous that no one of them, or no small group, has an appreciable influence on the price or on the volume supplied or demanded. **21**

The coal market is a competitive market, in this technical sense, and so are the markets for wheat and for most agricultural products. The markets for manufactured goods are typically not competitive, and the market for automobiles certainly is not competitive, no matter how vigorously Ford and General Motors may compete. As we shall see, the car market is oligopolistic.

In a competitive market, each seller can ignore the effects of his own actions on his competitors, and therefore on the price. So, he regards the going price as a given datum, and sells as much as he can or finds profitable at that price. We have already discussed at some length the operation of this type of market.

A monopoly is a market in which all, or virtually all, of the commodity is provided by a single seller.

The market for electric power in your city is undoubtedly a monopoly. Nylon was a monopoly for several years after it was first introduced. But aside from localized (and generally regulated) monopolies and monopolies of recently patented articles, this market form is rare—indeed, it is illegal.

A monopoly does not have a supply curve of the sort we have been discussing. A monopolist does not sit back and see what the price is before he decides how much to produce; rather, he decides on the price, and does so in the light of the volume of demand he expects at that price and the cost of producing that volume of output. The behavior of a monopolistic market is therefore fundamentally different from the behavior of a competitive one. We shall study monopolistic markets further in Chapter 6.

The most prevalent market form in this country is oligopoly.

An oligopoly is a market in which there are but a few firms, each of which recognizes that its actions have a significant impact on the price and supply of the commodity.

A list of oligopolistic products would include cameras, cans, computing machines, copper, and so on, and you can make such a list for any letter of the alphabet, including x. Almost all manufactured goods (except textiles and clothing) and most minerals have oligopolistic markets (coal is exceptional in this respect)— hence this market form is extremely important for understanding the operation of the economy. It is also extremely complex, for an oligopolist must balance three kinds of consideration in making his decisions: the demand curves for his product, his costs of production, and the reactions of his competitors. This market form also will be discussed further in Chapter 6.

TIMING AND DYNAMICS

Market adjustments, we repeat, take time. In our discussion of the coal market, we noted that mine operators can change the output of coal quite readily, but that most coal users have little choice but to continue using coal at customary rates until they can change their equipment. In other markets, the speed with which producers and consumers can respond to price changes differs—and, quite clearly, these speeds have much to do with the behavior of the market.

Farm products are an interesting example. A farmer cannot know the price that his current crop will bring at the time he plants it; he must base his decision largely on the price of the previous season's crop. Thus, if demand conditions remain stable, one season's price determines the next season's volume. The workings of such a market are illustrated in Fig. 2-6, which shows supply and demand curves for fresh cauliflower in a local market. The demand curve has the conventional interpretation—e.g., it shows that at a price of 5¢ a pound, around 112,000 pounds will be consumed in this market. The supply curve is a bit different; it represents farmers' responses to *this* season's prices. For example, if this season's crop sells for 5¢ a pound, farmers will plant only 90,000 pounds *next* season.

Now suppose that in some year (Year 1), the price was 5¢ a pound, so that 90,000 pounds were planted and harvested the following year (Year 2). What will the price be in Year 2? The forces of demand and supply will be at work, but the ordinary supply curve will not be effective because it represents reactions that cannot take effect until Year 3. In Year 2 the supply is 90,000 pounds, neither more nor less (abstracting from the possibilities of import and export), and the price must be such that consumers will wish to buy that amount. The effective supply curve, accordingly, is the vertical line labeled "market supply" in the figure. The effective equilibrium price is 6¢ a pound, the price at which the market supply will be taken.

At this point the ordinary supply curve takes over. A price of 6¢ a pound induces a planting of 99,000 pounds to be harvested in Year 3. In Year 3 the drama will be reenacted with a market supply of 99,000 pounds, leading to a price of 5.5¢ a pound, and so it will go. If the reader traces through a few more steps of the sequence, he will see that the price and quantity converge on the crossing point of the supply and demand curves: 96,000 pounds, selling for 5.8¢ a pound.[3] The intersection of the demand and supply curves is now truly an equilibrium, one (and

[3] This upshot is not inevitable. If the demand curve were much steeper (i.e., if consumers were less responsive to price changes), a crop below the equilibrium would cause such a sharp rise in price that the next crop would be farther above the equilibrium than the first crop was below. Prices and quantities in such a market would gyrate wildly without ever attaining equilibrium.

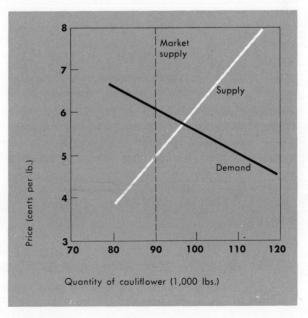

FIG. 2-6 Temporary and long-run equilibria for a market crop. Available supply determines temporary equilibrium price, which influences next season's supply in accordance with the supply curve.

this is the point of our example) that has been reached via a succession of *temporary* (single-year) equilibria, each demarcated by the intersection of the demand curve with the market-supply line.

This behavior of a simple agricultural market is actually an exaggerated instance of the way in which the markets for most commodities grope toward their equilibria. At each instant in this agricultural market, there were two supply "curves" rather than one: the market-supply "curve" (a vertical line), which determined the current price, and the sloping supply curve, which described the farmers' response to that price. In the same way, in markets for other commodities there are always two supply curves: a *short-run* supply curve, and a *long-run* supply curve.

> The short-run supply curve for a commodity shows the quantity that producers will provide in response to each price, using the plants and equipment currently available.

From the viewpoint of the cauliflower farmers, the market supply is depicted by the short-run supply curve, which takes the form of a vertical line because the farmers have no option in any year but to offer the quantity already planted. But manufacturing firms, like the coal mine operators discussed earlier, can vary their outputs in response to current market prices. Instead of being indicated by a vertical market supply line, the market for a manufactured commodity has a short-run supply curve with some slope to it, representing the extent to which output can be varied without changing the plants and equipment operating in the industry. Fig. 2-7 shows such a situation, with short-run supply curve No. 1 representing the responses of producers using the plants and equipment existing as of some particular date. The intersection of this short-run supply curve with the demand curve determines a temporary equilibrium level of prices and sales, as in the cauliflower example.

It is clear that when a temporary equilibrium has been attained, further adjustments of a more important kind may be induced. Established firms may find that plant enlargements would be profitable at the equilibrium level of sales. The level of profits may in fact be so high that new firms will be induced to enter the industry. Adjustments of these types are included in the long-run supply curve.

> The long-run supply curve shows the amount of a commodity that will be offered at each price when a triple adjustment has been accomplished: (1) each firm is producing the most profitable quantity at that price in the light of the current capacity of its plant; (2) each plant is of the size that permits the production of its current output at lowest cost; and (3) there is no tendency for firms to enter or leave the industry.[4]

A long-run supply curve is shown in Fig. 2-7. The ultimate equilibrium position of the market is given by the price and quantity at which the long-run supply curve and the demand curve intersect. The process by which the market works toward this equilibrium position is very similar to the adjustment of the cauliflower market, except that instead of planting different quantities in response to different short-run prices, the producers of nonagricultural commodities respond by changing the capacities of their factories (or whatever). The process of long-run adjustment merits detailed analysis, and this it will receive in the next chapter.

SUMMARY

In this chapter we have examined, in a preliminary way, the forces that

[4] An analogous distinction can be made between short-run and long-run demand curves (consider the case of coal consumers), but it plays a less important role in economic analysis.

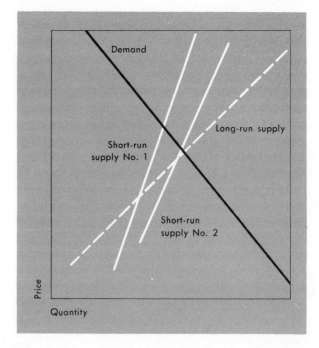

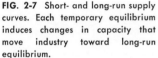

FIG. 2-7 Short- and long-run supply curves. Each temporary equilibrium induces changes in capacity that move industry toward long-run equilibrium.

explain the above-stated tendency. The demand curve illustrates the fact that the amount of a commodity that users wish to buy is influenced by its price. The supply curve shows that the amount of a commodity that suppliers find it profitable to produce and sell also depends upon the price. The price at which these two curves cross is the one at which producers are just willing to satisfy consumers' wishes. This price is called the equilibrium price, and to it there corresponds, on either curve, the equilibrium quantity. At this price, and this price alone, purchasers can buy the amount they wish, and producers can sell the amount they find profitable (as called for by our general definition of equilibrium).

A change in the underlying conditions of either supply or demand is reflected by a shift in the corresponding curve. When one of the curves shifts, its point of intersection with the other, and the equilibrium price and quantity, change too. When these curves are known, therefore, the consequences of a change in underlying conditions can be predicted. But extreme caution must be used in applying this method of prediction to underlying changes that affect simultaneously a substantial proportion of the individual markets in an economy.

The conceptual apparatus just sketched applies particularly well to competitive markets (those in which there are large numbers of sellers). It must be modified substantially before being applied to a monopolized market (one with only a single seller) or to an oligopolistic one (with only a few dominant firms).

Equilibrium analysis predicts certain adjustments to changes in supply and demand conditions, but says very little about how long those adjustments will take. The speed with which producers and consumers respond to price changes is important; on the side of the producers it gives rise to the distinction between short-run and long-run supply curves.

Behind the Supply Curves:

Competitive Markets

CHAPTER THREE

In Chapter 2 we learned that the supply curve is one of the two factors that determine the price of a commodity and the quantity traded. It follows that to understand what determines prices and quantities in an industry we must understand what determines its supply curve.

The supply of a commodity is the total amount offered by all the firms that produce it. It is the result, therefore, of decisions made in individual firms. So to explain a supply curve we must explain how an individual firm decides on the volume of its output —and this is the main topic of the present chapter. It is an easy step to proceed from the decisions of an individual firm to the supply curve of an industry as a whole.

Our analysis of the decisions of an individual firm will rest on the assumption that a firm ordinarily strives to maximize its profits. Though this assumption may seem trivial, it is really a bold simplification. In the first place, what are a firm's profits? We shall define:

> A firm's profits are the excess of the value of the things it produces over the costs incurred in producing them.

But, in actuality, profits cannot be measured by any such simple comparison. For example, when a firm is founded its operating costs may be greater than its sales for a year or more, but it would be naive to say, "The firm is losing money." Actually it is merely spending money to become established, so that it can earn profits in our simplified sense of the term. Furthermore, any firm is a complex entity that does *not* act consistently in accordance with this or any other simple assumption. It and its managers have their own peculiar "personalities" that play a part in determining its

26

decisions. Many advertising agencies will not accept liquor or cigarette advertising, though these are two of the most lucrative branches of the business.

Nevertheless, profits as we define them are one of the main considerations that virtually all firms attend to when making decisions. When we take an industry as a whole, the effects of individual peculiarities and temporary circumstances largely cancel out, and the industry behaves much as if every firm in it were striving single-mindedly to maximize its profits. It is well to be aware that we have made a simplification, but useful (and hopefully not misleading) to make it.

When a firm decides how much to produce under given market conditions, it takes two kinds of consideration into account: how the market (its customers and competitors) will respond to its decision, and how that decision will affect its costs. The market response depends largely on the structure of the industry—on whether it is a monopoly, an oligopoly, or a competitive industry. This chapter and the next will be devoted to firms in competitive industries; other market types will be discussed in Chapter 6. Thus we are now concerned with the decisions of competitive firms and, in particular, with how these decisions affect their costs, and how costs affect these decisions.

To put things in a slightly different way: to explain the supply curve of a commodity, we must first explain the supply curves of the individual firms that produce it.

> An individual firm supply curve shows the amount of a commodity that a single firm would like to produce and sell at each possible price.

In a competitive market no single firm exerts an appreciable influence on the price. Therefore it is a fair assumption that the quantity that a firm will supply at a given market price is just the quantity that will afford the greatest profit when sold at that price. So our task reduces to finding the most profitable quantity for the firm to provide—and we do this by means of a method called *marginal analysis*. To apply this method we consider any possible quantity of output and ask whether profits could be increased by producing one more unit. We also ask whether profits could be increased by producing one less unit. Only if the answer to both of these questions is negative can the assumed quantity be the profit-maximizing one.

The heart of marginal analysis is the behavior of costs. If the quantity produced is increased by one unit, the value of sales will increase by an amount equal to the price of the product. Whether profits are increased or not depends on whether producing the additional unit increases costs by more or less than the price of the product. So the effect on costs of producing various quantities of output is the key to the decision. We therefore turn to the analysis of costs.

FIXED COSTS AND VARIABLE COSTS

It is useful to divide all the expenses of operating a firm into two broad classes: *fixed costs* and *variable costs*.

> Fixed costs include all kinds of expenses that remain substantially the same whatever the level of output.

The most important fixed costs in a firm are those entailed by the ownership and maintenance of its plant and equipment. These include the interest on the capital tied up or borrowed, the rental value of the land occupied, the gradual wearing out or depreciation of its buildings and machinery, insurance, real-estate taxes, and the like. These expenses are incurred month after month whatever the level of operation of the firm's plant or plants, and even if they are closed down.

The second important category of fixed costs comprises the general expenses of management. The executive staff and other key personnel, and the accounting department, the purchasing department, the personnel department, and the other central functions of the firm must all be paid for, and their costs do not vary much whether the firm is running full-tilt or on short shifts.

Variable costs include all kinds of expenses whose level depends significantly on the rate of output.

The wages of production employees paid by the hour or piece are an important component of variable costs. Salesmen's commissions, the costs of raw materials, purchased parts, power, shipping, and storage and insurance of inventories are all of this general type because their levels are very sensitive to the rate of output and sales.

HOW COSTS VARY WITH OUTPUT

When a firm changes its rate of output, its variable costs naturally change in response. But the costs do not change in any very simple way; their behavior depends on all the factors that affect the firm's efficiency, and it so happens that a firm's efficiency varies with the level of its output. Generally speaking, firms tend to be inefficient both at very low and at very high rates of production. The best way to see why this is, and how it affects costs, is to trace through a typical example.

Table 3-1   HOW COSTS VARY WITH OUTPUT IN A HYPOTHETICAL FIRM

Monthly Production (Units)	Fixed Cost ($/month)	Variable Cost ($/month)	Total Cost ($/month)	Average Cost ($/unit)	Marginal Cost ($/unit)
100	1,000	900	1,900	19.00	—
200	1,000	1,600	2,600	13.00	7.00
300	1,000	2,200	3,200	10.67	6.00
400	1,000	2,800	3,800	9.50	6.00
500	1,000	3,400	4,400	8.80	6.00
600	1,000	4,050	5,050	8.42	6.50
700	1,000	4,750	5,750	8.21	7.00
800	1,000	5,550	6,550	8.19	8.00
900	1,000	6,500	7,500	8.33	9.50
1,000	1,000	7,650	8,650	8.65	11.50
1,100	1,000	9,050	10,050	9.14	14.00

Table 3-1 shows how costs might vary with output in a hypothetical manufacturing firm. The first column shows the possible levels of output per month, on the assumption that decisions are made for batches of 100 units each. The second column shows the fixed costs, which are $1,000 a month at all levels of output. This $1,000 pays the rent on the plant, interest on borrowed investment, taxes, insurance, executive salaries, and other items that do not vary with changes in the level of output. The third column shows the variable costs for each level of output: wages of hourly employees, raw materials, and other types of expenditures that directly reflect the level of production in the plant. The remaining columns are derived from these.

Now let us consider how these costs are influenced by the level of output. At the very lowest level, variable costs amount to $900 a month, so that total costs (the sum of fixed and variable costs) are $1,900 a month (fourth column). Since 100 units are being produced, the cost per unit, or *average cost,* is $19 (fifth column). The last column will be explained immediately.

If, now, the rate of output is increased to 200 units a month, fixed costs will not be affected, but variable costs will increase to $1,600 a month, shown on the second line of the variable-cost column, and total costs increase to $2,600. The increase in cost imposed by the second batch of 100 units is therefore $700, or $7 per unit. This figure is entered in the last column, labeled "marginal cost." For purposes of interpretation, this marginal-cost column is the most revealing one in the table.

Perhaps we had better pause here to define explicitly three concepts that we shall be using repeatedly. The first definition is obvious:

> The total cost of any level of output is the total expense of obtaining it. It is the sum of the fixed costs and the variable costs at that level of output.

The second definition is almost as obvious:

> The average cost of any level of output is the total cost divided by the output. In other words, it is the per-unit cost.

The third definition is more novel:

> The marginal cost at any level of output is the increase in total cost required to increase output by one unit from that level.

These three cost concepts are illustrated by the computations in Table 3-1. The figures given there for total and average costs follow the definitions exactly; the marginal-cost figures are only approximations, however, because the data do not show how much costs would change if output were altered by a single unit. The information is provided for batches of 100 units, so we have estimated the marginal cost to be one-hundredth of the addition to total costs caused by increasing output by one batch. (The data that businessmen and economists have to work with are frequently this crude—sometimes cruder.)

The mathematical relationships among total, average, and marginal costs are explained in the appendix to this chapter. Here we want to concentrate on how all of them evolve when the level of output changes.

The active component of total, average, and marginal costs is variable costs. Notice that according to the table the first 100 units required variable costs of $900, but the second 100 units added only $700 to that amount. Why should the second **29** 100 units require less by way of man-hours, raw materials, and other variable inputs than the first? The answer is that once the work has been set in motion for manufacturing the first 100 units of a commodity, a great deal of the work required for the second 100 units has already been accomplished. The purchase orders have been written, the job assignments have been made, the machines have been set up and adjusted.[1] All that is needed to increase the output is to write the orders for larger quantities and to let the machines run somewhat longer.

Continuing with the table, we see that the average cost when 200 units a month are produced is $13. This can be computed by dividing the total cost ($2,600) by the number of units produced.

The third batch of 100 units adds $600 to the cost of operation, bringing variable costs to $2,200, total costs to $3,200, and the average cost to $10.67. The marginal cost of producing the third batch is $6 per unit, which is a lower figure than that for either of the preceding batches, and one indicative of still further economies through increased mass production. (These come about because production can be organized more efficiently as the level of output increases: men can be assigned to more specialized jobs, and the different phases of the work can be better coordinated, with less slack, waste, overlap, etc.)

The fourth and fifth batches of 100 units cause the same increase in costs as the third, indicating that all the advantages of mass production have been gained at the output of 300 units a month. The fourth batch, though raising variable cost to $2,800 and total cost to $3,800, continues the decline in average cost; and the fifth batch, which again raises variable and total costs by $600 each, causes the average cost to fall even lower. (Why does average cost keep on going down although marginal cost is holding steady?)

With the sixth batch, however, a critical change occurs: this batch adds $650 to the variable and total costs, indicating a new marginal cost of $6.50 per unit. The cause of this jump in costs can be traced to difficulties that are beginning to arise on the production floor. Every plant has a certain capacity or rate of output that it can conveniently maintain. Oftentimes this economical capacity can be stated explicitly in numbers (as are the capacity of a power plant, and the load and speed restrictions assigned to an aircraft)—but these are seldom truly rigid figures; stated capacities of plants more often than not can be exceeded. The trouble is that when this is done, operating costs are likely to rise sharply.

Indeed, the marginal costs in a plant are likely to begin to rise well before its theoretical capacity is reached, and that is what we observe in the table. It is easy to see why this should be so. When a plant's output is comfortably below its capacity, every facility is in ample supply: there is plenty of room to work in and plenty of storage space to keep tools and materials just where they are needed; and machines can be shut down regularly for oiling and maintenance because there are reserve machines to take their places. (By the same token, production schedules are easy to keep even if a machine breaks down, because the reserve equipment *is* on hand.) But even before the nominal capacity of a plant is reached, this luxurious slack begins to disappear. Shelves and work-spaces become crowded, tools have to be kept in inconvenient places, parts begin to get lost and broken. When a single machine breaks down the work schedule may be seriously disrupted. Men

[1] Job printing provides a striking example. For a small number of copies, nearly all the cost is for setting the type and making the press ready. The number of copies can be increased simply by using more paper and running the press longer, with no increase in the heavy preparatory expenses. Nearly all production processes display this same distinction between setting-up costs and running costs.

and machines stand idle waiting for delayed subassemblies, thus delaying later stages of the production process. Inferior, standby machinery is brought into use. Some work has to be done on overtime. In short, costs rise (marginal costs, that is) —at first almost imperceptably, but then by leaps and bounds—as the sources of annoyance, inconvenience, and waste take more and more wind out of the sails of increased production.

Typical of the complaints when this state of affairs is reached are two reported in a prominent business paper:

> We are working 24 hours a day and in some cases six days a week ... costs are rising faster than sales. Not only must we pay heavy overtime, but inflated production schedules are causing more defective parts that have to be either reworked or scrapped.
>
> Where we should keep standby equipment for short runs, we've got to put it in the mainstream, and this pushes costs up.... Maximum capacity is not the most efficient rate—if we had our choice we'd drop back.[2]

All these sources of expense are reflected in the marginal-cost column of the table. The increase from 500 to 600 units a month causes only a little disruption: marginal cost rises there only 50¢ a unit. But the step from 700 to 800 units is more costly, and thereafter marginal costs rise swiftly indeed.

Now follow down the rest of the table. As marginal costs rise, the increase in variable and total costs accelerates and the decline in average cost decelerates; in fact, the decline comes to a full stop and then reverses itself.

2 *The Wall Street Journal,* September 16, 1965, p. 1 (slightly paraphrased).

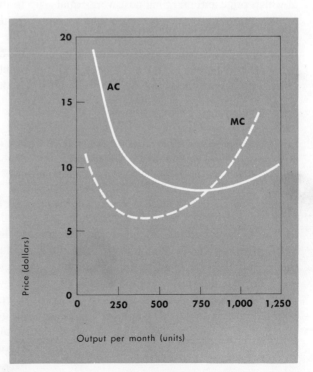

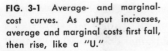

FIG. 3-1 Average- and marginal-cost curves. As output increases, average and marginal costs first fall, then rise, like a "U."

The relation of costs to the level of output is displayed most vividly by a graph of the cost curves, such as Fig. 3-1. The last two columns of Table 3-1 are plotted in that graph, and the tendency of average costs first to fall as output increases, and then to rise, is clearly shown. This tendency arises, as we have seen, from a contest between two conflicting forces. At low levels of output, variable cost per unit is low because each worker is able to work efficiently without encountering congestion or delays. But fixed costs per unit are high because the expenses of providing the fixed facilities are spread over a meager output. At the other end of the scale, fixed costs per unit are low but the inefficiencies of working in a congested plant push variable costs way up. Somewhere between the two extremes lies the happy medium where neither fixed costs per unit nor variable costs per unit is as low as possible, but the sum of the two is. This happy medium plays an important role in our subsequent analysis.

THE SUPPLY CURVE FOR AN INDIVIDUAL FIRM

Now that we have seen how a firm's costs are influenced by the level of its output, we have done most of the work required to understand its supply decisions. Remember that the firm is seeking the level of output that will afford it the largest profit when it sells its products at market prices. Which output this is can be determined by comparing the marginal-cost curve with the market price. Suppose, for example, that at the ongoing level of output the marginal cost is less than the market price. Then it would pay the firm to increase its level of output by one unit at least, because the increase in expenses (= marginal cost) would be less than the amount that the resultant output could be sold for (= price). In fact, it would be best for the firm to continue increasing its output until it reached the level at which price and marginal cost were equal—up to this point, each unit of increase would add more to sales revenues than to costs. On the other hand, if the marginal cost at the ongoing level of output is greater than the price, the firm could increase its profits by reducing its level of output by one unit at least, for then the reduction in monthly expenses would be greater than the resultant reduction in the value of sales. In this case the firm would be best off if it reduced its output to the level at which price and marginal cost were equal. Taking these two cases together, we conclude that:

> The most profitable level of output for a competitive firm is the one at which the marginal cost is equal to the market price.

The output that maximizes profit at any market price can be found by a direct computation; this is done in Table 3-2 for a price of $10 a unit. There the value of sales (= $10 × the output) is shown in the second column, total cost according to Table 3-1 is shown in the third column, and monthly profit (the difference between sales value and total costs) is in the last column. A glance shows that 900 units a month is the most profitable output at this price.

To find the most profitable level of output by direct computation, a table similar to Table 3-2 would have to be constructed whenever the market price changed. But a table, or graph, of marginal costs gives the correct level without any additional calculations. The marginal-cost column of Table 3-1 shows that output can be increased from 800 to 900 units at a marginal cost of $9.50 a unit.

Table 3-2 RELATION OF PROFITS TO OUTPUT
IN A HYPOTHETICAL FIRM (Price = $10 per unit)

Monthly Production (Units)	Sales Value ($)	Total Cost ($)	Profit ($)	Monthly Production (Units)	Sales Value ($)	Total Cost ($)	Profit ($)
100	1,000	1,900	900 *	700	7,000	5,750	1,250
200	2,000	2,600	600 *	800	8,000	6,550	1,450
300	3,000	3,200	200 *	900	9,000	7,500	1,500
400	4,000	3,800	200	1,000	10,000	8,650	1,350
500	5,000	4,400	600	1,100	11,000	10,050	950
600	6,000	5,050	950				

* Loss

At a market price of $10 a unit, that increase would be worthwhile—in fact, it should increase profits by 50¢ × 100 = $50 (check this on Table 3-2). But the marginal cost of the next batch is $11.50 a unit, which is not worthwhile at that market price. Hence the profit maximizing output is found without any calculation to be 900 units.[3]

It is clearly more convenient to determine the levels of output that firms will offer at various prices by using the marginal-cost data rather than direct computation, and just as accurate. As we reasoned above, the quantity that a firm will offer at any market price is the quantity for which the marginal cost is equal to that price. In other words, the firm's marginal-cost curve is also its supply curve. This is why the marginal-cost curve is so important. This firm's supply curve is shown in Fig. 3-2.

It is worth noting that the most profitable level of output depends on prices as well as on costs, and therefore is not necessarily the level for which average cost is lowest. In this example, average cost is lowest at an output of 800 units a month, where it equals $8.19 a unit. The most profitable output when the price is $10 a unit is 900 units a month, with an average cost of $8.33. (What will be the average cost when the price is $12 a unit?)

All the foregoing deals with profitable states of affairs. But if the price were lower than the lowest possible average cost, the firm would have to lose money. For example, there is no possible output at which the illustrative firm could cover its costs if the price were $8 a unit. Our reasoning applies nevertheless: losses are inevitable in such a case, but they will be as small as possible at the output for which marginal cost equals the price, an output of 800 units in this instance. There are, however, prices so low that if they reigned it would not be worth while for the firm to produce at all. The price of $6.75 is such a price in our example. If that were the market price and if the firm produced 600 units, its sales revenue would be $4,050, which would just cover the variable costs at that level of output (see Table 3-1). At any other level of output, variable costs would be greater than sales revenue at a price of $6.75 or less. Look, for example, at the variable costs for an output of 1,000 units. They are $7,650, which is considerably more than

[3] Notice that in this solution the marginal cost is not exactly equal to the market price. Exact equalities are a luxury reserved to mathematicians and theorists; businessmen and practical economists have to be content with approximations.

33

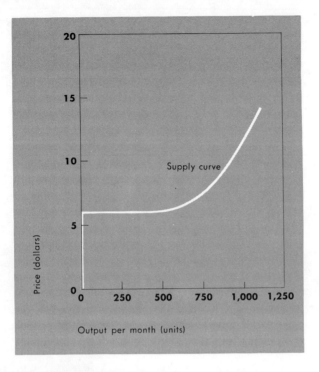

FIG. 3-2 Individual firm's supply curve. It coincides with the firm's marginal-cost curve for prices above the lowest possible variable cost. For lower prices the supply offered is zero.

1,000 times $6.75. Accordingly, at that price and at lower ones the firm will not offer any supply.

Thus our conclusion that a firm's supply curve is the same as its marginal cost curve is valid for all prices that are high enough to cover the variable costs of production at some level of output. At lower prices the firm will not offer any supply.

THE SUPPLY CURVE FOR THE INDUSTRY

The firm's cost curves determine its supply curve, i.e., the amount it will supply at every possible price. (Actually, its marginal-cost curve is the *same* as its supply curve unless the price is so low that variable costs cannot be covered at any level of output. At such low prices, the firm produces nothing.) The firm's supply curve, in turn, helps determine the industry's supply curve, for the supply of a commodity at any price is simply the sum of the offerings at that price of all the firms that produce it. This makes it easy to construct the supply curve for an industry if we know the supply or cost curves of some typical firms in it. In conjunction with our previous reasoning, this fact leads to an important conclusion:

The price of a product sold in a competitive market tends to be equal to the marginal cost of every firm in the industry or, in short, to the marginal cost of producing that product.

This is so because every firm in the industry will offer the quantity for which its marginal cost is equal to the common market price. However, if the quantities offered in response to the market price do not add up to the amount demanded at that price, the price will change (as we have seen in Chapter 2), and the offerings will change accordingly. When equilibrium is again established, the cost of an additional unit produced by any firm will then be equal to the market price.

But be warned that this conclusion is not valid for other than competitive markets, as we shall see presently.

THE PROBLEM OF THE LONG RUN

In summary, then, both the firm's and the industry's supply curves result from profit-maximizing decisions of businessmen according to the principles just described. The supply offered by the industry in response to any market price is just the sum of the supplies of the firms in it, each producing the amount for which the marginal cost is equal to that market price. This behavior determines the point on the supply curve corresponding to that price.

If the quantity thus offered corresponds also to the point on the demand curve for that price, consumers will be satisfied and that market price will persist. Otherwise the kinds of adjustment described in Chapter 2 will ensue until a price is established at which supply and demand are equal. In this situation each firm is making the highest possible profits given the market price, consumers' demands are being satisfied, and, also important, the total output of the industry is being produced at the lowest possible cost given the current outfit of plant and equipment in the industry. This is so because when marginal costs are the same for all firms in the industry, the industry's costs cannot be reduced by shifting some of the production from one firm to another. In other words, the industry's production task is distributed among the firms in the most efficient manner, and without any centralized direction.

But this is only a temporary achievement. The market processes we have discussed lead the industry to make the best use of its current stock of productive equipment. But that stock of equipment may not be appropriate to the current state of demand: the industry may be either over-equipped (as in the case of coal) or, more usually in a growing economy, under-equipped (as in the case of color television). When an industry's productive capacity is insufficient, the case on which we shall concentrate, other market forces operate to bring its capacity into line with demand.

It is obvious that when the demand for a commodity is greater than the industry can meet without taxing its facilities, the established firms tend to enlarge their plants and new firms are likely to be attracted to the industry. It is not so obvious that the signals and incentives provided by competitive markets lead the industry toward a state of long-run equilibrium in which the industry has the productive capacity required to satisfy the demand for its product at the lowest possible cost. Our objective, now, is to see that this is the case.

Long-Run Cost Curves

An industry's capacity expands in either or both of two ways: established firms may grow and new firms may enter. Both of these modes of expansion depend on the relationship between the size of a firm and its costs of production. This relationship requires us to consider a new kind of cost comparison. Up to now we have been studying how costs change with output when the same plant is used for

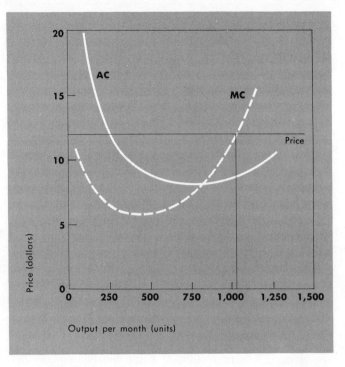

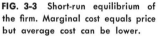

Price (dollars)

Output per month (units)

FIG. 3-3 Short-run equilibrium of the firm. Marginal cost equals price but average cost can be lower.

all levels of output. Now we must shift our attention to how the costs of producing a given output change when the plant itself can change. This leads us to the concept of long-run cost curves.

Consider a firm in short-run equilibrium, as in Fig. 3-3. When the price is $12 it makes its greatest profits by producing 1,050 units a month. But its average costs are not as low as possible there (they are lowest at an output of 800 a month), and its marginal costs are rising steeply. We know that this is because some of its facilities are being pushed beyond their most efficient operating levels. This leads us to suspect that 1,050 units a month could be produced more cheaply in a some-what larger plant. The technical possibilities might be as indicated in Fig. 3-4, where the cost curves from the previous figure have been reproduced (and labelled "O" for old) and some new cost curves (labelled "N" have been added) to repre-sent the costs of production in a plant designed for an output of 1,050 a month.

Three features of the new cost curves should be noted. First, they are lower than the old ones for high outputs because the effects of plant congestion have been reduced. Second, the new average cost curve is higher than the old one at low outputs because the larger plant entails higher fixed costs. (These two com-parisons show that when a firm enlarges its plant it incurs increased fixed costs in order to reduce its variable costs at high levels of output.) Third, the average cost of production in the larger plant at its designed level of output is the same as the average cost in the smaller plant at its most efficient level of output. This some-times happens, but by no means always, and we shall have to consider the various possibilities below.

If the price of the product is $12 and expected to remain so, the firm illus-trated could reduce its average costs and increase its profits by expanding its plant to the larger size, and every foreman, department head and customer who is vexed or discommoded by the current inadequate plant would be pressing it to do so. How large a plant would it be most profitable to acquire? Obviously, a plant in which the current and expected level of output (the same, because the firm is in equilibrium) can be produced most economically. On the assumption that this plant will be acquired we can define average long-run costs as follows:

A firm's long-run cost for producing any level of output is the cost of producing that output in a plant specifically designed for it. The long-run average cost is the long-run cost divided by the output, or the long-run cost per unit.

In the case illustrated the long-run average cost is slightly over $8 per unit at all levels of output; it does not show the rising tendency that this short-run average cost does. The implication is that larger plants can be built and operated with no loss of efficiency. Accordingly, this is an instance of *constant long-run costs,* which will be discussed further below. The entire long-run average cost curve, in this instance, is simply a horizontal line drawn through the bottoms of the two short-run average cost curves that are shown.

Long-run cost curves have no simple relationship to the short-run curves that we discussed before. The short-run curves describe the costs of producing various

FIG. 3-4 Effect of expansion of firm. Average- and marginal-cost curves both change. Average cost is lower for high volumes, and the supply at current prices increases.

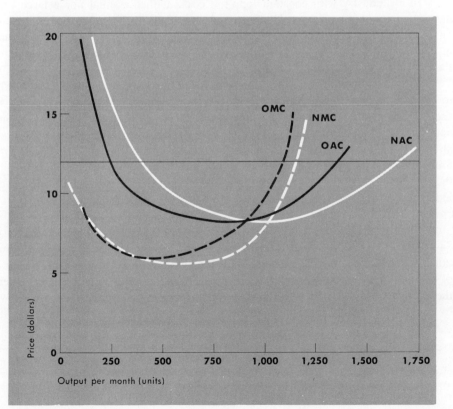

outputs in a given plant, whereas we are now concerned with the effects of changing plant size and design.[4] Long-run cost curves are what businessmen have in mind when they plan new facilities. They start by estimating their likely levels of sales and output, and then plan the facilities that will operate at those levels as efficiently as possible.

A firm is out of long-run equilibrium when its current average costs are higher than those that could be attained in a plant adapted to its current level of output or, in other words, when its current average costs are higher than its long-run average costs. The response of a firm, and an industry, to being out of long-run equilibrium depends on the shape of the long-run average cost curve. Three cases have to be distinguished.

Constant Long-Run Costs. The case of constant long-run costs has already been illustrated. It arises in many small and medium-scale manufacturing industries where plant expansion takes the form of replicating existing facilities. A large cotton mill is very much like a small one, except that it has more spindles. If a small mill is being overloaded, expanding it will permit average costs to be reduced. But the average costs of the enlarged plant at its most efficient level of operation will be about the same as those of the smaller plant operating at its most efficient level. The common sense of this is that twice as many men using twice as many spindles with twice as much cotton can make twice as much thread —doubling output by doubling the amount of every input leaves average costs unchanged.

In an industry with constant long-run costs neither a small nor a large firm has any particular advantage. Such an industry tends to be made up of a large number of firms of varying size. When the industry expands, the established firms in it grow and it is easy for new firms, usually of small to middling size, to enter the industry and compete on equal terms with the old ones.

Increasing Long-Run Costs. In some industries it is not possible for a firm to grow by acquiring new facilities that are as productive as the ones already in use. Mining is a case in point. A mine can increase its rate of output by digging new shafts, but these are liable to be less rich or less easily worked than the ones already operating. Law firms encounter a similar problem. A successful law firm finds difficulty in growing because it cannot attract personnel of the high quality that originally distinguished it. And there are a considerable number of other such industries. Where this occurs the firms are said to experience *increasing long-run costs.*

Figure 3-5 illustrates the behavior of costs in an increasing-cost industry. Short-run average-cost curves for plants of three sizes are shown. (There are some other data which can be disregarded for the moment.) $AC1$ is the average-cost curve of a small plant, which is most efficient at an output of 250 units a month, where the average cost is $10.20. The average costs for a middle-sized plant are shown by curve $AC2$. This plant is most efficient at an output of 750 units a month, with

---

[4] It is not even true that the bottom of a short-run average-cost curve indicates the average cost of producing that output in a plant of the most appropriate size. Two different concepts are involved: one is the output at which a given plant operates most cheaply in terms of average cost; the other is the plant at which a given output can be produced at the lowest average cost. The plant whose lowest average cost occurs at 1,000 units a month is not necessarily the same as the plant that can turn out 1,000 units a month most cheaply.

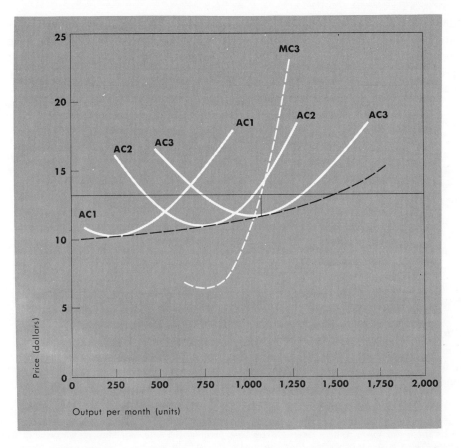

FIG. 3-5 Short-run and long-run cost curves for an increasing-cost industry. The lowest achievable average costs are higher in large plants than in small ones.

an average cost of $10.90. The large plant represented by *AC*3 produces most efficiently at 1,050 units a month, where its average costs are $11.60. Notice that even at their best the large plants cannot produce as cheaply as the small plant at its best but that, nevertheless, they are more economical at large outputs. Thus, a firm that expects a large volume of sales may have a large plant.

The dashed curve is the long-run average-cost curve, showing for each level of output the average cost when the product is produced in the best plant for that output. For example, if a firm expects to produce 750 units a month, it should construct the plant with the cost curve *AC*2, which touches the long-run average-cost curve near that level. Notice that the short-run average-cost curves lie entirely above the long-run average-cost curve. (Why?)

You might expect that firms tend to be small in industries with increasing long-run costs, since small firms can afford to undersell large ones. There is some tendency in this direction. But the same factors that make it hard for established firms to grow impede the entrance of small competitors. If an established mine cannot find an additional rich vein of ore, neither can a newcomer. Thus, in such industries, growth takes place by increasing firm size as much as by the entrance of new, small firms.

Decreasing Long-Run Costs. In many manufacturing industries, in transportation, and in some other fields, the techniques used by a large firm are radically

39

different from those available to small enterprises. Automobile manufacture is a dramatic and famous example. Practically speaking, no small automobile manufacturers exist in the United States. They simply could not afford the expensive presses, special-purpose automatic machine tools, or automated assembly lines that the giant firms employ. Where there are real advantages of mass production, so that large plants with intricate machinery can undersell smaller ones, there are *decreasing long-run costs*.

The short-run and long-run average-cost curves for such an industry are illustrated in Fig. 3-6. The curve labeled $AC1$ is the average-cost curve for a small plant that operates most efficiently at an output of 550 units, when its average cost is $8 a unit. $AC2$ is the average-cost curve of a middle-sized plant that can produce 900 units a month at an average cost of $4.70. The third cost curve is for a large plant that can achieve average cost of $3 a unit for volume of 1,350 a month. The dashed line is the long-run average-cost curve. It shows, for example, that an output of 750 units a month can be produced most economically in a plant with average-cost curve $AC2$, where the cost will be $5 a unit.[5] Similarly, every other point on this dashed curve shows the average cost of producing the stated output in the best possible plant for that output.

Large firms are the rule in decreasing cost industries. Table 3-3, compiled by Professor Joe S. Bain, shows the situation in a number of industries. Notice that in the gypsum, cigarette, and typewriter industries a single firm, to be fully efficient, must be large enough to supply a fifth or more of the entire national market. Two consequences follow. It is almost prohibitive for a new firm to enter such an in-

[5] A small paradox: The middle-sized plant is the best one for producing 750 a month (at $5 a unit), but it is not the best one for producing 850 a month although its average costs there are lower (about $4.70). The best plant is the one, not shown, whose short-run average-cost curve touches the long-run curve at 850 a month.

FIG. 3-6 Short-run and long-run cost curves for a decreasing-cost industry. Firms with large plants can sell at lower prices than smaller firms.

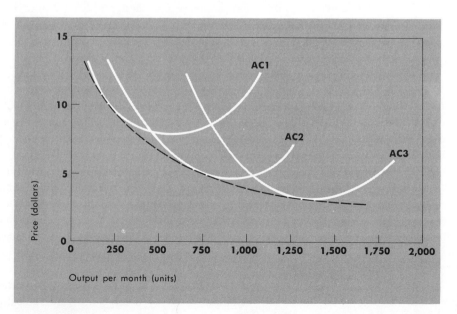

Table 3-3 PERCENTAGE OF MARKET SUPPLIED
BY MINIMUM-SIZE EFFICIENT FIRM

Industry	Percentage
Gypsum products	22-33
Cigarettes	15-20
Typewriters	10-30
Tractors	10-15 *
Copper	10
Steel	2-20
Soap	8-15
Automobiles	5-10 *
Fountain pens	5-10
Rayon	4- 6 *
Canning, Petroleum refining, Flour, Distilled liquor, Metal containers, Farm machinery, Tires and tubes, Shoes, Meat packing	3 or less

  * Size of efficient plant; minimum efficient firm may be larger. (The minimum size required for a firm to be efficient is different in different industries, but as a rule the firm rarely is large enough to supply more than a minor share of the market.)

Source: Joe S. Bain, *Barriers to Competition* (Cambridge: Harvard University Press, 1956), p. 86.

dustry; the requisite initial investment is too forbidding. Consequently, growth takes the form of increase in the size of existing firms almost exclusively. Second, competition cannot survive. The handful of giants who can undersell all prospective competitors constitute an oligopoly. The behavior of such industries will be discussed in Chapter 6.

An actual long-run average-cost curve, for the cement industry, is shown in Fig. 3-7. Each dot shows average costs in some plants of similar size. Small plants, with outputs below 500 barrels a year, are 50% more expensive, per unit of output,

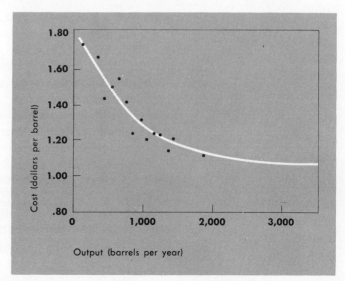

FIG. 3-7 Long-run average costs in the cement industry. Costs are significantly higher in plants with capacity less than 1,500 barrels per year than in larger plants. (Source: U.S. Tariff Commission. Reported by John M. Blair, "The Relation between Size and Efficiency in Business," *Review of Economics and Statistics*, XXIV, 1942, p. 129.)

than the large plants, with outputs above 1,500 barrels a year. After that level the decrease in costs appears to level off, as indicated by the curve drawn through the empirical data. Thus this is a decreasing-cost industry for small- and middle-sized plants, and a constant-cost industry for larger sizes. This general behavior is quite typical.

LONG-RUN SUPPLY AND EQUILIBRIUM

We have now listed the possible modes of behavior of long-run costs, and the technological circumstances that determine it. If long-run costs continue to decrease until individual firms are large enough to supply an appreciable share of the market, competition tends to break down, resulting in market conditions that we shall describe in Chapter 6. Now we consider how long-run equilibrium is attained in the other two cases.

When a firm expands in response to an increase in demand, it is likely to acquire the plant that can produce its current output at the lowest possible cost, as determined by the long-run average-cost curve. Thereafter its output in response to any market price will be decided from the cost curves applicable to the enlarged plant. The implications of this can be seen in Fig. 3-4. We may suppose that the firm has built the new plant in response to a market price of $12, at which it offered 1,050 units a month in accordance with the marginal-cost curve of the old plant. The new plant certainly produces 1,050 units more cheaply than the old one (compare the average-cost curves at that output) but also it has a new marginal-cost curve. If the price remains at $12, the firm will now offer not 1,050 units a month but more like 1,200, in accordance with its new marginal-cost curve. So, first, the firm's supply curve has moved, and, second, the new plant is likely to prove inadequate since it was not designed for 1,200 units.

Of course, the price is not likely to remain at $12. New firms will be entering the industry, others will be expanding their plants too, thereby moving their supply curves and the supply curve of the industry. The short-run equilibrium price resulting from the industry's new supply curve will be somewhat lower than $12. But even so, the new plant of Fig. 3-4, operated in accordance with its marginal-cost curve, will be used to produce more than its designed output, which sets up pressures for further enlargement. This process of growth, in a constant-cost industry, will not stop until the firms have grown enough and sufficient new firms have entered so that there is an industry supply curve that intersects the demand curve at a price of $8.10, which we have seen to be the long-run average cost for all outputs. This will be the price then, in long-run equilibrium, which is the status when every firm has the plant in which its current output can be produced most cheaply.

In a constant-cost industry, therefore, the price will gravitate toward the long-run average cost, which is the level of the (horizontal) long-run average-cost curve. The price will not be affected by the state of demand except to the extent that when the industry grows it bids up the prices of some of its factors of production, thus raising the level of the average-cost line. The prices of the products of such industries need not increase in the long run, even though the demand for their products grows.

In an increasing-cost industry the price in the long-run *is* affected by the state of demand, although firms behave in the manner described above. Suppose, in Fig. 3-5, that the price is $13.20 and that a firm has acquired a plant with cost curve $AC3$. The marginal-cost curve for that plant has been indicated (curve $MC3$). The assumed plant turns out to be the appropriate one for that price; it was carefully drawn so. The firm will neither increase its output from its current plant nor increase its plant capacity unless the price increases.

The contrast, then, between constant-cost industries and increasing-cost industries is this: A constant-cost industry will produce any desired output at a price equal to its (constant) long-run average cost. In the long run its supply curve is, in effect, a horizontal straight line. But an increasing-cost industry has a rising supply curve of the sort we are familiar with, even in the long run. If demand grows, its price must rise in the short run, and will not fall entirely back to its former level in the long run.

Agriculture is the leading instance of an increasing-cost industry, and helps us to understand the significance of increasing costs. When the output of wheat (for example) increases, land less and less well adapted to wheat growing is turned to that crop. This means that each additional ton of wheat produced requires more by way of labor, fertilizer, and other variable inputs than did its predecessor. The marginal cost per ton, which reflects the requirements for variable inputs, is consequently unavoidably high. The high marginal cost and price then indicate the high resource requirements of additional wheat, and discourage additional consumption in the interest of sparing these resources for use in the production of other products. Average cost remains below marginal cost because it is an average of the costs of producing wheat on the best land, on the worst land in use, and on all intermediate grades.

In general, the fact that marginal cost exceeds average cost in the long-run equilibrium of an increasing-cost industry is consistent with economic efficiency. It reflects the increasing requirement for variable resources imposed by each additional unit produced in such an industry.

In summary, we can think of long-run supply curves. Each point on such a curve shows the supply that the industry would offer in response to a given price, when the firms of that industry had had time to make the long-run adjustments just described. The long-run supply curve for a constant-cost industry is just a horizontal straight line. For an increasing-cost industry the supply curve rises with the price, in the usual manner. In either case, the point where this supply curve crosses the demand curve establishes the long-run equilibrium price and quantity, toward which the industry gravitates. When the market price equals the equilibrium price, each firm is producing at the level where its marginal cost equals that price also. At this point, the aggregate cost of producing the output is as low as possible considering the plant and equipment of the industry as given. In the long-run equilibrium position, no firm could reduce its costs by either increasing or reducing its plant. The industry has then the most efficient possible outfit of equipment for producing its output.

THE CONCEPT OF COST

Thus far in this chapter we have used the word "cost" as if everyone knew what it means. But the concept is really more subtle than you might think, as every accountant soon learns. We cannot in this little book go into all the intricacies of the problem of cost, but we must touch upon a few essentials.

One aspect of the problem is that the costs incurred by a business firm are not the same as its expenditures; many expenditures do not correspond to costs. For example, the price of a machine purchased to be used for many years is not part of the costs of output for the year during which it was bought. What *is* part of that year's costs is the *depreciation* of the machine—the decrease in the value of the machine caused by its application to that year's output. Although in principle this may seem clear enough, in practice it is very hard to estimate how much the value of a machine, or any other durable asset, is reduced by its use in any one period.

There are other expenditures, of the same general nature, where of even the principle is not so obvious. Take advertising, for instance. Expenditures for advertising not only help to increase current sales, but also have lasting effects which are likely to contribute to future sales. Accountants invariably treat advertising as a current cost—but is it? Or take for example the expenses of establishing a firm. When a firm is new or has recently introduced a new product, its operating expenses are likely to exceed its sales revenues until it has had time to build up its clientele. We say, "The firm is losing money." But wouldn't it be more accurate to say that the firm is still investing? The initial "losses" are expected, and if the project is well conceived, every month that they are incurred helps build the firm's market and contributes to its ultimate profitability. On the other hand, there are many important costs that do not correspond to expenditures, or which are measured very inaccurately by cash outlays. The depreciation of plant and equipment that a firm has owned for some time is a leading instance. Accountants always include depreciation among costs.

There are also some genuine costs that accountants do not include. Consider the following example. A farmer sells his produce for $200 a month more than the total of his cash expenses and reasonable depreciation on his farm equipment. He could, however, rent his land to a suburban developer for $300 a month. Is he making money by operating his farm? Clearly not. In fact, he is paying $100 a month for the privilege of farming, and any set of accounts that tells him otherwise is misleading. Proper accounting would include among his expenses the $300 a month that occupancy of the land costs him, and would then show that he is losing $100 a month in spite of the fact that his cash receipts exceed his disbursements.

Now this farmer is not a rare fellow. Every firm has its own funds invested, funds that could be loaned out at interest, or otherwise used to produce income for the owners, if the money weren't tied up in the business. Those funds are just like the farmer's land, and the income that they could earn, if not used in the business, is part of the cost of operating the business. But accountants don't include this foregone income in their books, because it is invisible. [6]

[6] This quirk of accounting has an implication for tax policy. When a firm borrows money to invest in its business, the interest on the loan is a tax-deductible expense. When it invests its own or stockholders' money, no tax deduction is permitted for foregone interest. This presents firms with an incentive to invest with borrowed funds instead of with their own capital.

In unincorporated businesses, the wages of the owners often are not included among the bookkeepers' records of expenses. The fact is, they are every bit as much expenses as are the wages paid to the employees. If the owner did not attend to his business he could earn wages by working for some other firm. These foregone wages are a reduction in his income just as truly as the wages he pays to his employees.

All these invisible expenses, and others like them, are included in the economist's concept of *opportunity cost:*

> The opportunity cost of producing anything is the income that could be obtained by the most advantageous alternative use of the resources devoted to it.

This is the fundamental and correct concept of cost. It expresses the notion that the real cost of producing anything is the most desirable other commodity that has to be given up in order to produce it. Money values are not costs—but foregone commodities are. Money is therefore only a calculus for expressing the value of foregone commodities. This is true because (we repeat for emphasis) it is alternative commodities, not money, that we give up in order to produce the commodities that we obtain.

When we say costs, then, we mean opportunity costs, and when we say that businessmen react to costs, we give them credit for understanding the deficiencies in their official books of account. They deserve this credit, too: the farmer in our story, for example, is very likely to sell out when the developer makes his attractive offer.

In particular, average costs and total costs throughout this chapter should be interpreted as opportunity costs. They include the cost of keeping the capital tied up in the firm, the value of the time of the managers, and sufficient payment for everything else used by the firm so that it would not be worthwhile to use it elsewhere. Many opportunity costs are fairly represented by market prices; this is true of the wages paid to employees and the prices paid for raw materials. But now we see that many genuine costs are *not* reflected in cash disbursements, and these we include in our concept of cost whether they are paid for in cash or not.

SOCIAL IMPLICATIONS

Let us set aside for the present the possibility that some of the industries in an economy may operate under conditions of decreasing costs, or may be not competitive for some other reason. Then the main results of this chapter can be expressed as two propositions:

> 1. In the short run, the price of every commodity and the marginal cost of producing it tend to be equal.
> 2. In the long run (to which the foregoing proposition also applies), every industry tends to have the stock of plant and equipment that makes the average cost of producing its output as low as possible.

45

These two conclusions are of the utmost importance because of what they indicate about the allocation of the economy's resources among its industries and commodities.

An economy might well be visualized as a vast workshop in which all commodities are produced and in which a great pool of resources is allocated among all the tasks of production. When the two conditions stated above are satisfied, this work is being organized as efficiently as possible—that is, the economy is obtaining the largest flow of commodities that can be obtained with the use of its resources. This is seen most clearly by considering the division of resources between two commodities that are not too dissimilar in their resource requirements. Let us consider automobiles and typewriters, both of which use steel, labor, power, and a large number of other inputs. In short-run equilibrium, the marginal cost of producing either will be equal to its price. Recall that the marginal cost of producing anything is the cost of producing one more unit with the given fixed plant, so that it consists entirely of the costs of the steel, labor, and other variable inputs needed for a unit increase in output. This means, for present purposes, that an automobile selling for $3,000 will require $3,000 worth of these variable inputs.

Now suppose that by the mandate of some high authority the production of automobiles were cut back by one unit and that the variable inputs that would have been used to make that automobile were transferred to the typewriter industry. Then, if a typewriter is priced at $300, those resources would suffice for producing ten typewriters at most.[7] This is true because if $3,000 worth of additional resources could be used to produce *more* than ten typewriters, the marginal cost of a typewriter would be *less* than $300. This transfer could not, then, increase the value of the goods in the economy. By the same argument, the same is true for a transfer of resources between any other pair of industries.

What's so good about that? Well, the price that an individual is willing to pay for a commodity is a measure of its importance or desirability to him. (Although common sense alone tells us this, we shall look into the matter further in Chapter 5.) In a somewhat looser way, the prices of different commodities also measure their social importance, even when they are not all purchased by the same individual. (This is discussed more thoroughly in Chapter 7.) So if it were possible to transfer resources between a pair of industries in such a way that the increase in the output of the receiving industry was valued more highly than the decrease in the output of the donating industry, then that transfer would be socially beneficial. And if no such transfer is possible, then the economy's resources are already distributed among industries in the most efficient manner.

That is the social implication of the first proposition. It tells us that the forces of competition lead to an optimal distribution of variable resources in the short run. It is important to note that to arrive at this conclusion we have had to exclude the possibility of decreasing-cost industries, in which competition is likely to break down.

Now we turn to the significance of the second proposition. Let us remain in the short-run framework and suppose that in the automobile industry the plant is the correct one for producing at lowest possible average cost, but that in the typewriter industry the plant is smaller than it should be. This would indicate that

[7] We say at most because the resources released by the automobile industry would probably not be of just the types that can be used to manufacture typewriters most efficiently.

somewhere along the line a mistake has been made in the direction of investment; a mistake, that is, from the social point of view.

We argue as follows. When the plant in an industry is such that average costs could not be reduced by changing its size, then the decrease in variable costs that would be permitted by a small investment in that industry would be just counterbalanced by the increase in fixed costs. Suppose, for example, that investment in the automobile industry had been $100,000 smaller than it was. The cost of the capital invested in an industry does not enter directly into the total cost of a year's operation or the average cost of a unit of its output. What enters directly is depreciation of the machinery, interest on the capital tied up, insurance, and similar expenses of maintaining and using fixed assets. Say that these come to $25,000 a year on the $100,000 investment. Then if the investment had not been made, these fixed costs would not have been incurred, and the variable expenses in the automobile industry would have been $25,000 a year greater than they are with the investment, since, by assumption, total costs cannot be reduced below their current level.

Now let us turn again to the typewriter industry, wherein we assume that average costs can be reduced by additional investment. If the $100,000 investment had been made in the typewriter industry, variable costs in that industry, at the same level of output, would fall by more than $25,000 in comparison with their level without the investment. That is where the mistake lies. If the $100,000 had been invested in typewriters instead of in automobiles, the society could have the same number of typewriters and of automobiles as under the assumed circumstances, with a smaller expenditure of variable resources in the two industries together. The resources so saved could be used to increase the output of typewriters, of automobiles, or of some third commodity.

This argument is of course perfectly general, because although it is especially easy to visualize the transfer of resources between two ferrous-metal fabricating industries such as typewriters and automobiles, the common pool of resources in an economy is so flexible in the long run that such shifts can be made between practically *any* pair of industries if the transfers are socially beneficial. But the second proposition, you will recall, asserts that competition leads to an allocation of investment among industries that does not permit any socially beneficial reallocation. Thus the automatic, competitive direction of investment is in the social interest.

Let us be careful not to claim too much, because we have not by any means covered all aspects in our discussions. We have neglected, for instance, the impact of decreasing long-run costs (though we shall go into that in Chapter 6). We have neglected some other things of importance, too. In particular, we have ignored the fact that things change—a fact that need not seriously diminish our enthusiasm for studying the competitive allocation of resources in the short run, but that does raise grave questions about the long-run equilibrium.

What we have found is that competitive inducements guide investment so as to make average costs in all industries as low as possible when those industries are using established techniques and confronting fixed demand curves. But demand curves are always changing, not only fortuitously, but also systematically as population grows and the economy becomes more wealthy. Techniques of production are **47** always changing, too, and so are the supply curves of the ultimate resources of production—labor, crude fuels, metallic ores, and the like. And the allocation of capital that is ideal for any one set of conditions will soon become obsolete and inappropriate. All we can conclude so far about investments (our analysis did not deal with the efficiency of investment in the dynamic context that actually exists) is that competitively guided investment will not be far from appropriate if conditions are not changing too rapidly.

In point of fact, businessmen have more wisdom (business acumen) than our simplified analysis gives them credit for. Certainly the considerations of immediate profitability that we have analyzed weigh heavily in their decisions, but, being forward-looking, they also take account of changes that they see imminent. We cannot demonstrate rigorously that businessmen's decisions are invariably ideal when they are caught up in a dynamic business context, but they are likely to be as sound as is humanly possible. In view of the limited ability of even shrewd businessmen to foresee the future, it seems unlikely that any other system for directing investments could perform better.

Some other necessary qualifications to the conclusions of this section will be pointed out in Chapter 7.

SUMMARY

This chapter has dealt primarily with four concepts: short-run costs, long-run costs, short-run supply, and long-run supply. From another point of view it has dealt with two kinds of decisions made by businessmen: how much to produce, and how large a plant to have. The four concepts play a central role in determining the two decisions.

The average cost of operating a plant at any level of output is the total expense incurred, divided by the volume of output. If the price of the product is equal to the average cost, all the expenses of production are exactly covered. But this does not mean that production is not worthwhile. Average costs should be interpreted to include the costs of keeping capital invested in the enterprise, wages sufficient to make participation worthwhile by the owners and everyone else involved, and payments for everything used in the enterprise high enough to attract it there. If the price is higher than the average cost, profits are being earned in excess of those necessary to induce the current level of production.

For technological reasons, average costs tend to be high both when a plant is being under-utilized and when it is being overworked; the average-cost curve has the shape of a "U." The cost of increasing the rate of output by one unit a month (or other time-period) therefore is different from the average cost; it is called the marginal cost. A firm's profits are greatest at the level of output for which the marginal cost is equal to the price. This, consequently, is the level of output that a businessman will select. It follows that the marginal-cost curve is also the short-run supply curve for an individual firm, and that the short-run supply curve for an industry can be found by adding up, for each price, the amounts that the individual firms will offer at that price according to their marginal-cost curves. The price at which this short-run supply curve intersects the demand curve is the short-run equilibrium price for the industry, and the corresponding quantity is the rate of output that the industry will provide when in temporary equilibrium relative to its current plant.

When the market price so established is greater than the lowest average cost at which firms can operate profitably, the firms will be operating at levels beyond the low points of their average-cost curves. They will be able to reduce their average costs (the sum of fixed and variable costs per unit) by enlarging their plants, and they are likely to do so. In the same situation, the firms will be earning profits above the minimum required to remain in the business—a circumstance that is likely to attract new entrants. In these conditions the output of the industry will increase, both because established firms are expanding and because new firms are entering. The upshot of this expansion depends on the shape of the long-run cost curves of the firms in the industry.

A firm's long-run average cost for any level of output is the average cost when that output is produced in the plant most appropriate for it. When that plant is being used, any further increase in plant size will increase fixed costs by at least as much as it reduces variable costs. The long-run average-cost curve for an individual firm in a competitive industry may be horizontal or it may rise, depending on whether the industry operates under conditions of constant or of increasing cost. If mass-production technology offers substantial advantages, the firms' long-run, average-cost curves are likely to be downward sloping, in which case competition will usually break down into oligopoly.

A firm's long-run supply curve is related to its long-run average-cost curve. The quantity that a firm will offer in the long run in response to any market price is the quantity for which marginal cost equals that price, when the marginal cost is computed for the plant that can produce that quantity most economically. The industry's long-run supply curve cannot be derived from those of the individual firms, however. Allowance has to be made for (a) the entrance and exit of firms in the long run, and (b) the possible effect of changes in the size of the industry on the prices of its purchased inputs. Whether the industry's long-run supply curve slopes upward or not, its intersection with the demand curve for the product determines the long-run equilibrium price and production level of its commodity.

Both the short- and the long-run equilibria of a competitive industry are positions of high economic efficiency. When all industries are in short-run equilibrium the marginal cost of producing every commodity is equal to its price, indicating that there is no social advantage to be gained by transferring variable resources from one industry to another, given their current outfits of plant and equipment. It is also true that when all industries are in long-run equilibrium, investment has been divided efficiently among industries, because then a transfer of investable resources from one industry to another will increase variable expenses in the industry that loses the resources by at least as much as it decreases them in the industry that gains, at constant levels of output. One of the main advantages of competitive markets is that they tend toward these equilibria.

Relations Among the Cost Curves

The three cost curves introduced in this chapter describe the same physical data and are therefore related mathematically. Let $TC(x)$ be the total cost of producing output x in a certain firm with a given plant. Then the average cost of output x, $AC(x)$, is defined as *the total cost divided by the amount produced,* or

$$AC(x) = \frac{TC(x)}{x} \tag{1}$$

Marginal cost, $MC(x)$, is defined, precisely enough for our purposes, as *the increase in total cost imposed by a unit increase in output.*
Therefore:

$$MC(x) = TC(x + 1) - TC(x)$$

Making use of equation (1) we can also write:

$$MC(x) = (x + 1)AC(x + 1) - xAC(x)$$
$$= x[AC(x + 1) - AC(x)] + AC(x + 1)$$

Hence:

$$AC(x + 1) - AC(x) = \frac{MC(x) - AC(x + 1)}{x}$$

Suppose now that output x lies in the range in which average costs are falling. Then the left-hand side of this equation is negative, implying also

$$MC(x) < AC(x + 1) < AC(x)$$

To put it literally: If average costs are falling, then marginal costs are less than average costs.

By similar reasoning, if average costs are rising, making the left-hand side positive, $MC(x) > AC(x+1) > AC(x)$. Thus, average costs rise when and only when marginal costs are above average costs.

Finally, from the facts that average costs are above marginal costs when average costs are falling, and average costs are below marginal costs when average costs are rising, it follows that the two curves must cross where the average-cost curve bottoms out—i.e., where average costs are at their minimum.

Behind the Cost Curves:

Production Choices and Costs

CHAPTER FOUR

We have just seen that the cost of producing a given quantity of a commodity depends upon the plant in which it is produced. It may be turned out in a small plant with low fixed costs and a great deal of hand work, or alternatively in a large, mechanized plant with high fixed costs and a small amount of labor. In the long run, when the firm can choose its plant, it will select the one in which production costs are lowest.

This choice between incurring fixed and variable costs is one instance of a problem that businessmen constantly face: how to produce their products as cheaply as possible. They search incessantly for economical methods of operation. This search results, of course, in efficient operation of their plants. But it also has two other consequences, which will be explained in this chapter. One result is the efficient distribution of labor and other resources among plants and industries (which is not the same thing as their efficient utilization within plants). The other is an impact, on the markets for labor and other resources, which helps determine wages and the prices that resources command. This chapter is devoted to the consequences of businessmen's searches for the cheapest methods of production. But first, we must describe the search.

FINDING THE CHEAPEST METHOD: AN EXAMPLE

Because every branch of production is based on some specialized technique, examples of production choices that are not entangled in technicalities are rather rare. But one class of pro-

51

duction problem is so frequent and important that it has a name, and it isn't very technical. This is the "lot-size problem," and we choose it as our illustration.

The issue is this: most manufacturing processes are carried out in "lots" or "batches" in which a number of identical articles are produced, after which the machinery used is cleaned up, readjusted, and prepared for the manufacture of something else. For example, a paint manufacturer will mix a certain number of gallons of one color, then clean his vats and use them to mix another color. Or a steel-rolling mill will produce a certain number of tons of one thickness, then stop, be readjusted, and be used for steel of a different gauge. This is the most common mode of operation in manufacturing.

Setting up equipment for a particular job is expensive, so it is desirable to produce a large lot once the machinery is prepared. On the other hand, storing things is expensive, so it is desirable to produce small lots frequently, in order to avoid having to store a large stock. The lot-size problem is the problem of finding the best resolution of these conflicting considerations.

To be specific, suppose that an electronic firm requires 500 chassis of a certain type each year (as a component for its final product) and that each chassis stored requires a square foot of storage space renting for $2.50 a year. If the chassis are produced in two lots of 250 each, the firm will have to rent storage space for 250 chassis, at a cost of $625 a year. Suppose that to set up the drills for manufacturing a lot of chassis (that is, a batch of 250) requires 10 hours of skilled labor costing $5 an hour, or $50 for each batch. Then, the setup and storage costs for two batches a year would amount to $625 + $100 = $725. The cost of materials, manufacturing labor, and so forth are irrelevant for this problem, since they are the same for 500 chassis irrespective of the number of batches into which they are divided.

Another possible choice is to make 10 lots of 50 chassis each. Then, storage space for only 50 chassis would be needed, costing $125, but there would be 10 setups, costing $500. The total cost for this choice would be $625. Clearly this is better than manufacturing two batches, but is it the best possible decision?

We analyze this problem by means of a convenient and flexible scheme.[1] Two resources are involved here: storage space and skilled labor. The amounts used can be represented in a graph (like Fig. 4-1), wherein the amount of labor is plotted vertically and the amount of storage space horizontally. Each point in the diagram represents a certain pair of amounts of the two factors. For example, point A represents 20 hours of labor and 250 square feet of storage space; point B represents 150 hours of labor and 40 square feet of storage.

Now, the desired 500 chassis can be produced by using 20 hours of labor and 250 square feet of storage space, or 100 hours of labor and 50 square feet of storage, or any of many other combinations.[2] The curve labeled "500" passes through all the combinations that just suffice for producing 500 chassis. Point A lies on this curve; point B, whose quantities are sufficient for 600 chassis, lies above it.

Such a curve is known as an *isoquant* (from the Greek *iso* = equal, and Latin *quantus* = how much).

---

[1] Actually, this is not the best method for solving this particular problem, but it is the most instructive for the purpose of economic analysis.

[2] In fact, any combination will do for which number of Square Feet × Hours of Labor = 5,000.

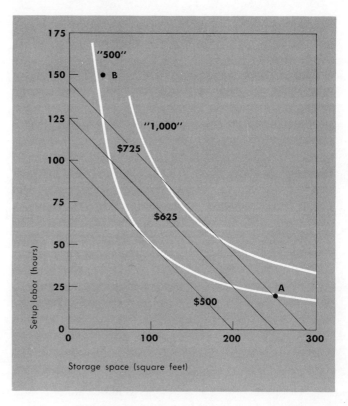

FIG. 4-1 Isoquant diagram for the lot-size problem. Two isoquants and three isocost lines are shown. The solution occurs where an isoquant touches an isocost line.

An isoquant for a given level of output is a specification of all the combinations of factors of production that are just adequate for producing that output.

An isoquant exists and can be drawn for every level of output. Two are shown in Fig. 4-1: the one for 500 chassis a year and the one for 1,000. Each isoquant displays graphically all the combinations of storage space and setup labor that can produce the specified output but no more. Our problem is to find the cheapest combination on the isoquant for 500 units.

Each point on the diagram has a certain cost of attainment. For example, point *A* costs $725: $100 for 20 hours of labor, plus $625 for 250 square feet of space. We can connect all the points that cost $725; this is done in the diagram by the line labeled $725. Such a line is an *isocost line*.

An isocost line shows all combinations of factors of production that cost the same amount in toto.

The isocost lines have a very easy formula. The equation for the isocost line for $725 is

$$2.5X + 5Y = 725$$

where X is the number of square feet of storage space and Y is the number of hours of setup labor. Similarly, the isocost line for any other level of cost will have the formula

$$2.5X + 5Y = \text{cost.}$$

Because the coefficients on the left-hand side are the same for all isocost lines, they form a family of parallel lines. Three are shown.

The problem is solved by finding the lowest isocost line—i.e., the lowest member of this family—that touches the isoquant for 500 units. This turns out to be the isocost line for $500 (look at the graph), which just touches the isoquant at the point representing 50 hours of labor and 100 square feet of storage space. Thus we have found the cheapest production plan and its cost.

This example, incidentally, throws additional light on why average costs fall as volume grows, until the plant becomes congested. With a little arithmetic (such as solving the same problem for a use-rate of 1,000 a year) you can see that the setup plus storage costs per unit produced diminish as the use rate grows. (We found them to be $1 per unit for a use-rate of 500 a year; they are about 71¢ for a use-rate of 1,000 a year). This contributes to the declining trend in average costs at low levels of output for all commodities produced in batches.

The cost curves in Chapter 3, of course, presume that the cost-minimizing problem has already been solved. That is, the cost used there for producing a specified output in a specified plant are the costs when the least expensive combination of variable inputs is used.

IMPLICATIONS OF THE SOLUTION

The batch-size problem illustrates some of the most fundamental characteristics of production. Everything that is produced requires the use of some inputs, or factors of production. If we know the technology of production and the amounts of the different factors available we can figure out the greatest amount of the product that can be made. But we cannot reason so sharply in the other direction: if we know the quantity of product to be manufactured and the technology, we cannot deduce unambiguously the amounts of the different factors that are required. Every product can be made in numerous ways, each requiring a different combination of inputs. This is where the isoquants enter: each isoquant specifies all the combinations of inputs that can be used to produce a given amount of a product within the framework of a given technology. Which combination will be used is a matter of choice, and businessmen normally select the cheapest.

In the batch-size problem the choice that ultimately determined the quantities of the two inputs takes the form of deciding on the sizes and frequency of the production batches. In other circumstances the details of the choice are very different. One additional example will help to indicate the variety of possibilities. In cutting cloth for clothing manufacture, the major factors of production used are cloth and cutters' labor. The critical man in the process is the pattern maker—his task is to arrange the pieces into which a bolt of cloth is to be cut so that the job can be done as cheaply as possible. If inexpensive cloth is being used, he arranges the patterns loosely so that the cutters can work quickly. If the cloth is expensive, he places the pattern pieces tightly together to reduce the amount of cloth wasted as trim and scraps. In the latter case the cutters have to work more slowly and carefully, but they use less cloth per garment. (An extreme instance of this trade-off between care and material occurs in diamond cutting, where days of planning may be lavished on a single uncut stone to make sure that as little as possible is wasted.)

We saw in an earlier chapter that electric power companies have to choose among different sources of power, and in the last chapter that every firm has choices between more or less elaborate fixed plant and variable costs. All these choices, and many others, have the same logical form. The resource inputs required by the alternative methods for obtaining a given output are specified by an isoquant. The combinations of different quantities of inputs that can be purchased for a given total expenditure are specified by an isocost line. The point on the isoquant that lies on the lowest isocost line gives the cheapest combination of inputs that can be used to produce that output. The method of production that requires this cheapest combination of inputs is the one that the businessman is likely to adopt.

This behavior is reflected in Fig. 4-2, which shows how industrial firms divided their purchases between electricity and gas in states where the ratio of the prices of these two sources of energy was different. Each dot in the diagram represents a state. The ratio of the price of a therm (100,000 BTU's) of gas to the price of a kilowatt-hour of electricity is plotted vertically; the ratio of the amount of gas used by industrial firms to their purchases of electric power is plotted horizontally. For example, the dot in the upper left-hand corner represents a state where a therm costs about 20 times as much as a kilowatt-hour. Industrial firms in that state use a minuscule amount of gas—perhaps 1% as much gas as electricity. At the other extreme there is a state where a therm costs only twice as much as a kilowatt-hour. The firms in that state use slightly more gas than electric power. The dots between the two extremes show the general tendency that we should expect: broadly speaking, the lower the ratio of gas to electric prices, the higher the ratio of gas to electric usage.

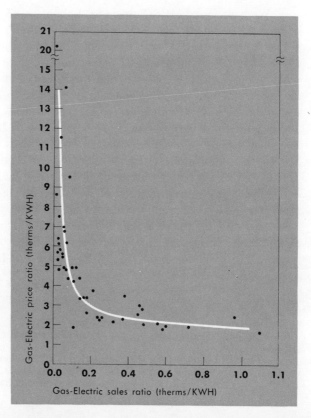

FIG. 4-2 Industrial use of gas and electric power, by states, 1961. Firms use more gas in proportion to electricity in states where the price of gas is lower relative to the price of electric power. (Source: J. R. Felton, "Competition in the Energy Market between Gas and Electricity," *Nebraska Journal of Economics and Business*, IV, Autumn, 1965, p. 7.)

SUBSTITUTION AND FACTOR PRICES

The best way to produce a given output clearly depends on the prices of the factors used, for these prices determine the isocost lines. We now have to express more specifically the relationship between the factor prices and the choice of input combination. The batch-size problem illustrates this relationship if we approach it from a slightly different point of view. We now apply to it the same strategy that we used in the last chapter when we wanted to find the most profitable output: the strategy of analyzing small, or marginal, variations in the decision.

Consider again the decision to manufacture two lots of 250 chassis each, the plan requiring 20 hours of setup labor per year. The amount of labor required could be reduced to 15 hours a year by producing 1½ batches per year.[3] Each batch would then have to contain 333 units, to meet a requirement for 500 units a year. Thus the amount of storage space would have to be increased from 250 square feet to 333 square feet. The effect of this change in production plan would be to substitute 83 square feet of storage space for 5 hours of setup labor without affecting the rate of output. The possibility of such substitutions of dissimilar factors of production is of the essence in keeping production costs down. It is expressed in general by the *marginal rate of substitution* of one factor of production for another, or *MRS* for short. Formally:

> The marginal rate of substitution of factor X for factor Y, written MRS(X for Y), is the number of units of factor X needed to replace one unit of factor Y with the rate of output remaining the same.

We have found MRS(Storage for Labor) = 83÷5 = 16.6 when 20 hours of labor and 250 square feet of storage are being used.[4] Though this substitution does not affect the rate of output, it is likely to affect the cost. In this case, saving 5 hours of labor saves $25, but adding 83 feet of storage space costs $83—clearly an unwise substitution. In fact, it indicates that the substitution should be made in the other direction; that is, it would be better to increase setup labor to 25 hours and reduce storage space to 200 square feet, which can be done by producing 2½ batches of 200 chassis per year. This would reduce costs by $125 − $25 = $100.[5]

The general principle at work here is that costs can always be reduced if the MRS at the combination selected is not equal to the ratio of the prices of the factors. This is easy to see. Suppose that the prices are p_x and p_y. A substitution that does not change the output consists of reducing the use of factor Y by one unit (saving p_y) and increasing the use of factor X by MRS(X for Y) units, which will cost p_xMRS(X for Y). The net result will be to reduce cost if the saving in expenditures on factor Y, or p_y, is greater than the offsetting increase in expenditures on factor X, amounting to p_xMRS(X for Y). Indeed, the net saving will be $p_y − p_x$MRS(X for Y).

---

[3] There is no reason to restrict ourselves to round numbers. One-and-a-half batches a year (of 333 chassis each) is the same as three batches in two years, and can support a use-rate of 500 a year.

[4] Our result is only approximate because the curvature of the isoquant introduces some error.

[5] The MRS derived from this substitution is 10. It differs from the previous one because, in effect, we are looking at the MRS corresponding to 25 hours of labor, though we are applying it in reverse. Each combination of factor quantities has its own MRS.

If this net saving is positive, then the use of factor Y should be reduced by one unit, at least, and the requisite number of units of factor X should be substituted for it. On the other hand, if the net saving is negative, costs can be reduced by increasing the use of factor Y and cutting back on the use of factor X. The only time when costs cannot be reduced is when the net saving is zero, or, equivalently, when

$$\frac{p_y}{p_x} = \text{MRS}(X \text{ for } Y).$$

This equation, then specifies the relationship between the prices of the factors and the marginal rate of substitution between them when the most economical combination is being used. We have arrived at an important general principle:

When the cost-minimizing combination of factors is used, the MRS of any pair of factors is equal to the ratio of their prices.

You can check this, if you like, by computing the MRS(Storage for Labor) at the cost-minimizing combination (50 hours, 100 square feet), but it is more instructive to confirm it graphically. Graphically, the kind of substitution we are considering consists in moving from one point to another on the isoquant for 500 units, since none of these substitutions changes the output. The MRS is the ratio of the changes in the quantities of the two factors; in other words it is the slope of the chord connecting the combinations before and after the change. For very small changes this chord is to all intents and purposes the tangent to the isoquant, and it is best to think of it as such. Thus the slope of the isoquant at any point is the graphic representation of the MRS there.

But the price ratio is the slope of the isocost line, and this also is easily seen. Suppose, as before, that the prices are p_x, p_y. If the firm buys one unit less of factor Y, it will have p_y more to spend on factor X without changing its total expenditure on the two factors. This amount will buy p_y/p_x units of factor X. The isocost line then moves p_y/p_x units to the right whenever it moves one unit down, and this is its slope.

So when the MRS is equal to the price ratio, the isoquant has the same slope as the isocost lines. We can now rephrase our conclusion to say:

The cost-minimizing combination of factors for any output is given by the point on the isoquant for that output at which the slope is equal to the slope of the isocost lines. At this point an isocost line will be tangent to the isoquant.

Figure 4-1 shows that this relationship holds for the lot-size problem. This problem, or any other one of the same type, can be solved by following the isoquant until we find the point at which it has the proper slope.

Businessmen, of course, do not follow isoquants, or even draw them. But they do, by their own devices, strive to minimize their costs of production. When they do so, no matter how, they arrive at a combination at which the relationships deduced in this chapter hold—at least approximately. That is why we are interested in these relationships.

THE "LAW OF DIMINISHING RETURNS"

Our whole argument and its conclusions depended heavily on the shape of the isoquant that we deduced for a very special problem. In particular they depended on the fact that the isoquant curved up so that its tangents lay below it. (Why was this important? Where would the cost-minimizing point be if the isoquants had a different shape?) In mathematical language, we found that the isoquants were *convex*.

Granting that the isoquants for the lot-size problem are convex, can we rely on finding that same property in general? There is no general principle that says we can. Whether the isoquants pertaining to any particular production situation are convex is a matter of fact that depends on the relevant technology. But there are good reasons for thinking that isoquants usually have this shape, and that is what we shall argue in this section. Actually, we shall argue it in two stages: first we shall explain the "law of diminishing returns," and then we shall derive from that "law" the convexity of isoquants in normal circumstances.

The "law of diminishing returns" is one of the oldest and most fruitful insights in economics. It arose from observation of the production conditions in agriculture. Suppose that a farmer is cultivating an acre but is using very little fertilizer. Then he is likely to obtain a very meager crop because of nutritional deficiencies in the soil. But if he applies a little more fertilizer, say 5 pounds per acre, the half-starved plants will show a sharp increase in growth. A second dose of 5 pounds will increase growth still further, but not as much as the first dose. As successive increments of 5 pounds each are applied, each will contribute less to growth than its predecessor, until finally, when the soil is provided with all the nutrients that the plants can take up, further doses are both figuratively and literally fruitless.

This sort of behavior is not peculiar to fertilizer; it is the same with seed, with water, with the labor of cultivation, and with every other input to agricultural production: whenever the amount of one input is increased, the first additions yield greater responses than the later ones. Nor is this phenomenon restricted to agriculture. Consider the cloth-cutting example. If a bare minimum of cloth is used, the patterns must be placed very close together and the cutters must work very slowly around awkward corners. If a bit more cloth is used, the worst corners can be eliminated and the output of the shop, per week let us say, will go up. Another bit of cloth will permit a little more improvement, but not as much as the first, because the worst impediments have already been eliminated. And so it will go as the amount of cloth is increased foot by foot, until finally the ultimate in convenience is achieved, and having more cloth is only a nuisance.[6]

Although these observations and many more like them do not constitute a proof of anything, they do suggest very strongly a general principle:

> If the amount of any one factor of production is increased in successive equal doses, the amounts of the other factors remaining the same, then successive increases in output will be obtained, up to some limit, but each increase will be smaller than its predecessor.

[6] This suggests another aspect of the "law of diminishing returns." If the amount of any one factor is increased without increasing the amounts of the others, it will eventually become deleterious. Too much water is a flood, too much fertilizer burns the soil, too much cloth becomes an unwieldy tangle. Then the returns to increases in the varying factor are worse than small; they are negative.

This is the "law of diminishing returns"—which, as you may already have surmised, takes quotation marks (instead of being capitalized or italicized) because it is not really a law; there are exceptions to it. Exceptions granted, however, sufficient universal truth remains within this "law" to have established it as one of the basic guides that determine the efficient use of economic resources. Indeed, if there is a single, key insight on which economic theory depends, this "law" is it.

The importance of the "law of diminishing returns" may be more properly emphasized by stating it in a slightly different way that has the advantage of introducing a very important concept, the concept of *the marginal product of a factor.*

> The marginal product of a factor of production is the increase in output that results when one more unit of that factor is employed, the quantities of all other factors remaining the same.[7]

The importance of this concept is that the marginal product of a factor measures its usefulness in terms directly pertinent to economic decisions. For instance, the cost of using an additional hour of labor is the hourly wage. The gain from using that hour, in a competitive industry, is the marginal product of labor (the amount of the product produced by that man-hour) times the price of the product. If the marginal product-times-price is greater than the hourly wage, profits can be increased by employing more labor. Very simple. Also very important, and we shall follow up its implications in a later section. Now we can state what the "law of diminishing returns" asserts about marginal products:

> As the amount of any one factor is increased, the amounts of all other factors remaining fixed, the marginal product of the factor that varies will fall.

The "law of diminishing returns" does not establish that isoquants are convex, since it deals only with the consequences of varying factor inputs one at a time— but it supports the belief that they are. Any of our examples will show why. In the cloth-cutting example, suppose that a choice has been made on the isoquant for some quantity, near the end representing high inputs of cloth and low inputs of labor, as at point A in Fig.4-3. If, now, the amount of cloth to be used per week is slightly reduced, the amount of labor remaining the same, the patterns can be arranged somewhat more tightly so as to keep the same number of cutters busy on the smaller quantity of cloth. Output per week will fall, because the cutters have to work a bit more slowly, but it will not fall much because the amount of cloth after the change is nearly as ample as it was before. This is in accordance with the law of diminishing returns. Graphically, the decrease in the use of cloth moves us to point A', on a lower isoquant than point A but not much lower.

If the original rate of output is to be restored by increasing the amount of labor, only a small increase in labor time will be necessary because the deficiency

---

[7] Students often become confused about the directions of the changes used in definitions like this one, and in the definition of the MRS. Why isn't the marginal product the *decrease* in output that results when one *less* unit of a factor is employed? The answer is that it doesn't make any difference. For small changes you get about the same result, in whichever direction you take the variation. So we shall not pay any attention to this distinction, and shall take the marginal product to be either the increase resulting from one more unit, or the decrease resulting from one less, whichever is more convenient at the moment. The same goes for the MRS, marginal cost, and other definitions relating to the effects of small changes.

to be made up is small and because, with so much cloth to work with, the additional cutters can still work fast. This also is in accordance with the "law of diminishing returns." Such a restoration returns us to the original isoquant at point *A"*. The two changes together constitute a substitution of labor for cloth along the isoquant. The chord from *A* to *A"* approximates the slope of the isoquant, or the MRS, which is seen to be high.

Contrast this with the same operations departing from point *B*, where the supply of cloth is already so short that a great deal of labor is required to attain the isoquant. Reducing the amount of cloth (i.e., moving from *B* to *B'*) now increases the amount of slow and delicate cutting and reduces the weekly output more than the reduction considered before. Point *B'* accordingly lies on a lower isoquant than point *A'*. The return to the original isoquant (at point *B"*) consequently requires a large increase in the use of labor, both because a large decrease in output has to be made up and because the output per manhour is low in that part of the isoquant. Hence the chord *BB"* is flat. All this means that as we move down an isoquant it becomes flatter, as drawn, or that it is convex.

This discussion indicates that the isoquants descriptive of cloth-cutting technology are likely to be convex; we cannot establish anything more than that. But since the influences that determine the shape of the isoquants in cloth-cutting are so similar in their general nature to the influences operative in other technologies, it seems reasonable to conclude that isoquants will in most instances have this same general shape.

FIG. 4-3 Effect of substitution between two factors. The marginal rate of substitution changes along an isoquant, making it convex.

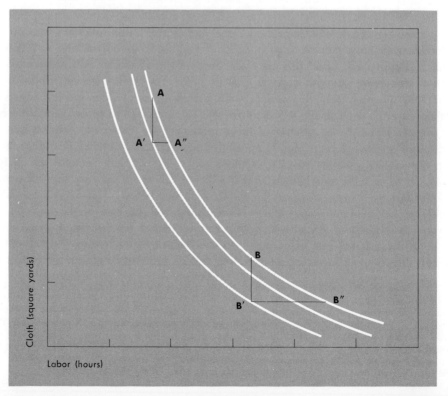

MARGINAL PRODUCTS AND FACTOR PRICES

The marginal rate of substitution between two factors is closely related to the marginal products of the two factors individually. We shall work out this relationship now, and then use it to get some new and useful formulas for the cheapest way to produce an arbitrary output and also for the most profitable output to produce.

Recall that the marginal product of a factor is the amount by which output would be increased if one more unit of the factor were employed, the use of all other factors remaining the same. The amount by which output would decline if one less unit of the factor were used, other inputs remaining unchanged, is approximately the same. We shall denote the marginal product of factor X by MP_x.

Now suppose that certain amounts of two factors, X and Y are being used, and consider the effects of varying their quantities. If the amount of Y is reduced by one unit, output will fall by MP_y units where MP_y denotes the marginal product of Y. Now suppose that the use of X is increased by u units. Output will increase $u\mathrm{MP}_x$ units if u is small enough so that the marginal product of X doesn't change appreciably as a result of the variation. The net effect on the output of these two changes is

$$- \mathrm{MP}_y + u\mathrm{MP}_x.$$

Finally, choose u so that the change in output is zero. We obtain

$$u = \frac{\mathrm{MP}_y}{\mathrm{MP}_x}.$$

But this is the marginal rate of substitution of X for Y, the number of units of X that can replace one unit of Y without affecting output. In other words:

> The marginal rate of substitution between two factors is the ratio of their marginal products.

That conclusion is true, mathematically, whatever combination of factors is being used. We found above that when the cost-minimizing combination is used, the MRS is equal to the ratio of the prices. Putting these two facts together we find that when the cost-minimizing combination is used

$$\frac{\mathrm{MP}_y}{\mathrm{MP}_x} = \frac{p_y}{p_x}$$

for any two factors of production. That is to say:

> When any quantity of output is being produced in the cheapest possible way, the marginal products of the factors used are proportional to their prices.

Let us check on this conclusion in the batch-size example. The cheapest combination for producing 50 chassis a year was found to be 50 hours of labor and 100 square feet of storage, i.e. to produce 5 batches a year. An additional square foot of storage would therefore permit batch-size to increase to 101 chassis, and output to be increased by 5 units a year. The marginal product of storage space is

61

5 chassis. If the use of setup labor were increased by 1 hour, the batch-size would have to remain at 100 but the number of batches could be increased to $5\frac{1}{10}$ per year. The increase of a tenth of a batch means that output would be increased by 10 chassis, which is thus the marginal product of storage labor. The marginal product of setup labor is thus twice that of storage space. Now, if you will look back at the data of the problem you will confirm that the ratio of their prices was $5.00 : 2.50 = 2$, just as our theorem predicted. The theorem holds whenever a cheapest combination of factors is used, which is a condition that businessmen strive to achieve.

An immediate consequence is that if output is to be increased by one unit or other small amount it doesn't matter which input is used to obtain the increase. For suppose that output is to be increased one unit by using more of factor X. One additional unit of factor X will increase output by MP_x units; therefore a unit increase in output requires $1/MP_x$ additional units of factor X. The cost of achieving the increase is then p_x/MP_x.

Similarly, if the increase in output were achieved by using more of some other factor Y, the cost would be p_y/MP_y. But our proportionality formula shows that these two costs are the same. You can verify this for yourself, using the data of the batch-size problem.

This finding ties right in with the analysis of costs in Chapter 3. There we defined the marginal cost of a commodity to be the cost of increasing its rate of output by one unit. Now we find that the marginal cost of a commodity is p_x/MP_x, where p_x is the price of any factor used to produce the commodity and MP_x is the marginal product of that factor. It doesn't matter which factor we use for this computation since the ratio is the same for all (when the least-cost combination is used). For example, taking factor X to be labor, the marginal cost of an electronic chassis when 500 are being produced is $5/10 = \$.50$.

Finally, we recall from the last chapter that when the profit-maximizing output is produced, the marginal cost is equal to the price of the product. Denoting the product's price by p_o this can be written:

$$p_o = \frac{p_x}{MP_x},$$

or more conveniently:

$$p_x = p_o MP_x.$$

Since this is a condition that businessmen aim to maintain, we conclude:

The wage or price of any factor tends to be equal to its marginal product times the product price, or to the value of its marginal product.

Hardly any principle in economics is more important than this one, for the simple reason that hardly any question that economists deal with is more important than the determination of the wages of labor and payments to other factors of production. We shall discuss it further below.

THE PRODUCTION FUNCTION

We have used three main concepts in this chapter: isoquants, marginal rates of substitution, and marginal products. All describe aspects of the broad relationship between quantities of inputs and quantity of output. They can be understood and remembered most easily by thinking of them in the context of this broad relationship, called the *production function.*

> The production function for any firm expresses its technology by stating the greatest output it can obtain from any possible combination of quantities of inputs.

A production function can be stated in many ways. It may take the form of a mathematical formula. An isoquant diagram, such as Fig. 4-1, is a method of expressing the production function, since the maximum output obtainable from any pair of input quantities can be read off it. Perhaps the most graphic way to show a production function, when only two inputs have to be considered, is to draw a "production hill." This requires three dimensions: one for each of the two inputs and one for the output.[8] Such a production hill is shown in Fig. 4-4. Quantities of two factors, *A* and *B,* are shown horizontally, the resultant output is measured vertically. The marginal product of *A* is shown by the steepness with which the hill climbs as you move from left to right, parallel to the *A*-axis. The marginal product of *B* is shown by the steepness of the hill as you move backwards, parallel to the *B*-axis. The hill shows the phenomenon of diminishing marginal productivity that we discussed above: it is steeper when the quantities of the inputs are small than when they are large.

The isoquant diagrams are, in effect, an alternative way to depict the production hill. You may have noticed that the isoquant diagrams are very similar in construction to the contour maps used by geographers to represent terrain features and, especially, altitudes. Just as the geographer does, we can visualize an isoquant diagram as the two-dimensional representation of a hill in which the quantities of two factors of production are plotted instead of latitude and longitude, and the quantity of output is plotted in place of altitude. The isoquant representation of Fig. 4-4 is shown in Fig. 4-5. There the isoquant for 200 units of output is shown,

---

[8] A production hill can be drawn only when there are two factors of production to be considered, but the concept of a production function encompasses any number of factors.

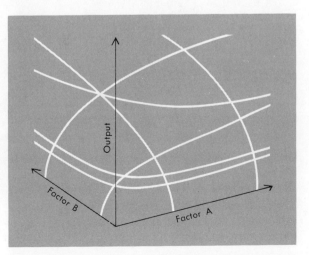

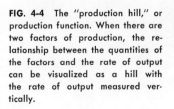

FIG. 4-4 The "production hill," or production function. When there are two factors of production, the relationship between the quantities of the factors and the rate of output can be visualized as a hill with the rate of output measured vertically.

and the isoquant for every 10 units thereafter, up to 390 units. Every fifth isoquant is emphasized for clarity.

One of the two salient features of this isoquant map has already been discussed: the isoquants are all convex. The other significant feature is that the isoquants are densely clustered toward the bottom of the "hill" and spread apart near the top. Every user of Geological Survey maps knows that tightly-clustered contour lines indicate a steep climb for him, while spread-out lines signify easy going. The interpretation of the isoquants on the production "hill" is similar: at the bottom of it a small increase in the use of either factor will increase output the 10 units from 200 to 210; output there climbs steeply in relation to input. At the top, however, a large increment in either factor is required to increase output those last 10 units from 380 to 390. There, the level of production climbs slowly in relation to increases in the use of the two factors.

Each of these isoquants corresponds to a certain total cost which could be ascertained by drawing in the isocost line tangent to it.[9] Where the isoquants are close together, the increase in total cost between any one and the one above it is

[9] The isocost lines have been omitted to keep the diagram uncluttered.

FIG. 4-5 Isoquant diagram to represent the production function. Each isoquant is an altitude contour of the production hill.

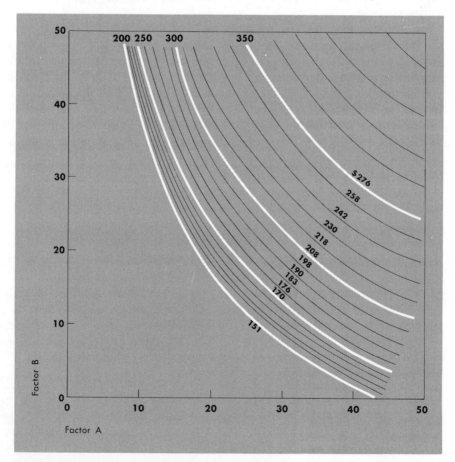

small. Since the isoquants are drawn for constant increments of output (10 units), this means that marginal costs are low. Where the isoquants are far apart, a large increase in total cost is needed to increase output by 10 units; marginal costs are high. Thus the spreading-out of the isoquants is another mode of expression for the increase in marginal costs at high levels of production.

To facilitate the following step, we have written next to some of the isoquants in Fig. 4-5 the total cost of attaining them.[10] Note that the increase in output from 200 to 250 units costs $19, the increase from 250 to 300 units costs $38, and the increase from 300 to 350 costs $68. Marginal costs are increasing as predicted. To find the best isoquant, or the best quantity to produce, we have only to compare marginal cost with the price of the product. Suppose, for example, that the price of the product is 70¢. We note from the diagram that the increase in output from 260 to 270 units costs $7, so that the marginal cost when 260 units are being produced is about 70¢. Then 260 units is the best output to produce, in accordance with the findings of Chapter 3.

Though the production function is a very informative concept as a theoretical tool, it is not of much value to the businessman in making his practical decisions. Even the smallest firm is too complicated to have its workings summarized conveniently in this form. For one thing, there is no such thing as a firm that uses one, or two, or a handful of factors of production. But, more fundamentally, the relationships between inputs and output in any actual firm are exceedingly complex. The batch-size problem with which we started is only a tiny part of the production function of the electronics firm. Similar problems arise in the fabrication of every component of its product. They arise even in the administration of the firm, but who can tell the relationship between the number of bookkeepers employed and the number of chassis that can be produced?

In practice, a businessman knows only a few bits and pieces of his production function; his foremen and department managers know other bits and pieces. All together they know enough to employ their resources relatively efficiently. And that is sufficient for our purposes, which are to explain the principles relating the use of factors to their market prices.

DEMAND CURVES FOR FACTORS

One of the main results we have obtained is the formula relating the price or wage of a factor to its marginal product and the price of the commodity produced:

$$p_o = p_x \mathrm{MP}_x.$$

This relationship explains the demand curve for factors of production, and therefore goes a long way toward explaining the prices of factors of production, of which the most important is wages. For suppose that the price of factor B of Fig.

[10] That is, the cost of the least-cost combination, using prices of $5 for factor A and $3 for factor B.

4-5 increases to $4. The isocost lines will become flatter [11] so that 18.7 units of factor *A* with 28 of factor *B* will no longer be the cheapest pair for producing 260 units of output. Furthermore, the cost of attaining each isoquant will be increased, so that 260 units will, in all likelihood, no longer be the most profitable level of output. We know that the first of these effects is sure to reduce the firm's use of factor *B,* and the second effect is likely to reinforce the first. Thus the firm will use less of factor *B* at a price of $4 than at a price of $3, and precisely how much less could be figured out from the firm's isoquant diagram by finding the most profitable production point corresponding to the new set of prices. (We shall not bother to do that.) Such calculations, performed for a variety of prices of factor *B,* would trace out the firm's demand curve for the factor.

What this all means is that if we had the firm's isoquant diagram, knew the price of the firm's product, and knew the price of factor *A,* then we could figure out how much of factor *B* it would use at every possible price for that factor. This would be the *firm's* demand curve for factor *B.* Making the same computation for all the firms in the industry and adding up the results, we could obtain the *industry's* demand curve for factor *B.*[12] Finally, making the same computation for all industries that use factor *B,* and adding up these single-industry demand curves, we could derive the *economy's* demand curve for factor *B.*

The economy-wide demand curve so deduced is half the explanation of the price of the factor (its wage, if it is a type of labor); the other half is the supply curve of that factor. Where these two curves cross would in the usual way determine the price of the factor.

The plan of calculation just described is impracticable on the face of it—but that's not the point. It does show that the price commanded by a factor is related ultimately to its marginal productivity reflected in the isoquant diagrams of the individual firms that use the factor. The foundation of the economy-wide demand curve for a factor is that every firm will use an amount of the factor at which the value of its marginal product is equal to its price. The activities of labor unions, the enforcement of minimum-wage legislation, and other such complications cannot alter this fact because they do not affect the demand curves for factors. Such devices for influencing factor prices change the supply curve, and thereby change both the price of the factor and the quantity employed, but the fact remains:

> The price of any factor of production (including labor) equals the value of its marginal product.

This statement is known as *the marginal-productivity principle of factor price determination.* It is a principle which should not be regarded as a complete explanation of the price of any factor of production—say, of wages. It asserts a significant equality between two economic variables but does not in itself explain either of them. What it does explain is the amount of a factor of production that will be used at any price for it—i.e., the demand curve for the factor. For, if the price of the factor is given, each firm will employ the amount of it at which the value of its marginal product (its marginal product multiplied by the price of its product) is equal to that factor price. The market price of the factor will be de-

---

[11] Neglecting, for simplicity, the fact that a significant change in the price of factor *B* would be likely to change the price of the product, and even that of factor *A.*

[12] Check for yourself what the isocost lines look like when the price of factor *A* is $5 and the price of factor *B* is first $3 and then $4.

termined by this demand curve working in the usual way, in conjunction with the supply curve for the factor.

Although the marginal-productivity principle just deduced is but half the explanation of factor prices, it is often useful on its own account. For example, one often raises the question, "Can unions raise wages?" In a certain sense they undoubtedly can. If factor B in our diagrams is a unionized craft, a sufficiently strong union could insist on a contract that would raise the wage from $3 to $4 an hour. But if it did so, the value of the marginal product of this craft at the level of employment corresponding to a $3 wage would be less than the current wage. Other factors would be substituted for this one and, since the wage increase would be likely to raise the marginal cost of the product, the level of output would probably fall. For both these reasons, members of the craft would be thrown out of work. At the same time, the increase in the wage would, if anything, increase the number of men desiring work in the craft. The union would then have difficulty in maintaining the increased wage, unless it could persuade employers to retain men whose marginal productivity was low (hence "featherbedding" rules), and could exclude nonunion members who wanted work in the trade (hence apprenticeship rules, closed-shop contracts, and similar devices). Clearly, strong pressures have to be resisted in order to maintain a wage substantially higher than what the value of the marginal product of the craft would be if all men desiring work in it were employed.

SUMMARY

The motivating idea of this chapter is that businessmen determine the cost of attaining any output by choosing the combination of factors with which to produce that output. Their range of choice is described by an isoquant, which shows the combinations of quantities of different factors of production required to produce the specified quantity of output. In general, the isoquant can be conceived of for any number of factors of production, but it can be shown graphically only for two factors, and we have concentrated on such cases.

Isoquants can be compared with isocost lines, which specify the quantities of different factors of production that can be procured at a constant aggregate cost. The cheapest combination of factors for producing a given output corresponds to the point where the isoquant for that output touches, and is tangential to, the lowest possible isocost line.

The slopes of the isocost lines represent the ratios of the prices of the factors of production. The slope of an isoquant at any point represents the marginal rate of substitution between the factors there—that is, the number of units of one factor needed to compensate for the loss of one unit of the other, leaving output unaffected. When the cheapest combination of factors is used to obtain any output, the marginal rate of substitution between any pair of factors is equal to their price ratio.

When the price of any factor rises in proportion to the prices of the others, the least-cost combination for any output will change. Less of the more expensive factor will be used in proportion to the others than in the preexisting least-cost combination.

The isoquant map, the diagram showing isoquants for different levels of production, is the fundamental datum underlying both cost curves and supply curves. It can be used to determine the most profitable level of output as well as the least-cost method for producing that output. The isoquant diagram is simply a convenient way of showing the production function when only two factors of production are under consideration. The production function incorporates all the technical data about production; it shows the greatest amount of output that can be obtained by the use of every possible combination of input quantities.

The marginal product of a factor is the increase in output that results when one more unit of that factor is used, all other factor quantities remaining the same. It, too, can be read off the isoquant map. When the least-cost combination of factors is being used, the marginal cost of the product equals the ratio of the price of any factor to the marginal productivity of that factor, this ratio being the same for all factors. This is so because the number of units of a factor required to produce one more unit of output, other factor quantities remaining constant, is the reciprocal of the marginal product. Multiplying the number of units of the factor required by the price of the factor gives marginal cost. The significant fact is that the cost of a small increase in output is the same no matter which factors are varied to secure it, provided that the starting point was the least-cost combination.

Even more can be said when the firm is producing the most profitable output in the cheapest way. Since under those circumstances marginal cost equals price, we can assert that a dollar's worth of any factor will produce a dollar's worth of output.

The marginal products of the factors are the foundation of the demand curves for them. If the price of the factor varies, the quantity employed will vary, too, so that in every firm that uses it, a dollar's worth of the factor will produce a dollar's worth of the product—or, in fancier language, so that the value of the marginal product will remain equal to the price of the factor. This is the basis of the marginal-productivity theory of factor pricing, which is useful in understanding wages and other factor prices even though it does not provide a complete explanation.

The "law of diminishing returns" helps justify the shapes of isoquants and isoquant maps. It asserts that the marginal product of any factor tends to decline when more of it is used in proportion to the factors that cooperate with it. Our explanation of the tendency of short-run costs to rise with increases in output is an instance of this general phenomenon. The convexity of isoquants in general is a consequence of this same principle.

Throughout this summary, and in fact throughout this chapter, we have indulged in some verbal shorthand. For example, we have stated firmly that the price of a factor is equal to the value of its marginal product. The truth is that this and many similar assertions hold only in certain restricted circumstances—though it should be emphasized that they are circumstances that competitive markets tend strongly to bring about. All these statements, in fact, are statements of equilibrium conditions (that is, of conditions that will obtain only *after* firms, their customers, and their suppliers have had time to adjust to changes in circumstances). This detracts somewhat from the exactitude of our assertions, but it does not diminish their importance.

Behind the Demand Curves

The past few chapters have explained the considerations that determine the supply of a commodity: the amount that will be produced and offered in response to any market price. But we should not forget that the main purpose of production is to satisfy consumers' wants. Now we turn to the study of demand, which is the mechanism by which consumers' wants and tastes find expression in the marketplace and thereby become known to producers. The importance of the demand curves is that they tell producers how strongly consumers desire each commodity, relatively to others. Just how consumers' desires find reflection in demand curves is what we now have to elucidate.

The demand for a commodity is the amount that purchasers choose to buy. It therefore depends ultimately on how consumers make up their minds, and on all the attitudes, customs, fashions, and other influences that affect purchasing decisions. Clearly, just what a consumer decides to purchase is a very complicated matter whose full explanation requires all the knowledge that psychologists, sociologists, and other experts on behavior can muster. Economists, however, do not purport to explain purchasing decisions in their full richness and complexity. They undertake a different task: without attempting to account for tastes, they ask how consumers with given wants and preferences allocate their expenditures among the different commodities that they might purchase. They ask also how changes in prices and in consumers' incomes affect this allocation. In short, they concentrate on only one factor that influences purchasing decisions: how much the commodity costs in relation both to the costs of other things and to what the consumer can afford. They do not do this because

69

prices are the most important influences on consumers' decisions (usually they are *not*), but because the consumers' decision to buy or not at given prices is the main channel by which consumers communicate their desires to the rest of the economy.

One consequence of this concentration is that economists ignore many aspects of consumers' decisions that are of engrossing importance to other people, such as sociologists and advertising experts. Some time ago, for instance, the psychologists who advise the tea importers' association concluded that tea sales suffered because Americans (in contrast to Englishmen) regarded tea as a sissy's drink. The tea importers consequently spent large sums trying to erase this "image" of effeteness associated with their product. Now, although the question of whether tea is a he-man's drink is undoubtedly important from some points of view, to an economist it is irrelevant simply because it throws no light on the operation of the economic system; he is willing to take such attitudes, preferences, and customs only as primary data. Taking such attitudes, etc., as given, his concern instead is with the answer to the question: How are consumers' decisions affected by changes in prices and in incomes? This shall be our question, also. We shall attempt in answering it to show how the economic system responds, within the limits of its productive capabilities, to give consumers what they want.

CHOICE BETWEEN TWO COMMODITIES:
UTILITY MAXIMIZATION

Our analysis begins with a very simple question. Supposing that a consumer has a given amount of money to spend, how should he divide his expenditures among different goods so as to achieve maximum satisfaction? In other words, what must he do to get the most for his money?

To answer this question, let us make up an example that we shall study in some detail. Mrs. X, a remarkably systematic housewife, has already decided to spend exactly $50 on frozen foods for the coming month. The question that now confronts her is how much of that to spend on meat (costing $1 a pound) and how much on vegetables (costing 40¢ a pound). Notice that the total amount she has to spend, and the two prices, delimit her range of choice. She could spend her whole $50 on vegetables (obtaining 125 pounds of them), or all of it on 50 pounds of meat. Of course, she is not very likely to do either of these; instead, she will probably buy some number of pounds of meat, say x (somewhere between 0 and 50), and some number of pounds of vegetables, say y (somewhere between 0 and 125), chosen so that her total bill will not exceed her limit of $50. That is, her choice can be described by two letter-symbols, x and y, delimited by the condition

$$x + .40y = 50$$

—a range of choice depicted by the straight line in Figure 5-1.

More generally, if a consumer has B to spend on two commodities whose prices are p_1 and p_2, his range of choice is given by all combinations of x and y, such that

$$p_1x + p_2y = B.$$

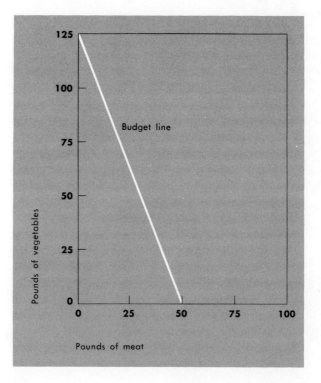

FIG. 5-1 A budget line. The budget line shows all combinations of commodities with the same total cost.

Such a range of choice, corresponding to a given budget and prices, is called a *budget line*.[1] The budget line shows how prices and the budget limitation jointly define the range of choice open to the consumer. Algebraically, this limitation is expressed by a linear equation; geometrically, it corresponds to a straight line. But the budget line gives no information about which pair of quantities, satisfying the budget equation, the consumer will choose.

Indifference Curves

Conceptually, we can split the problem of consumers' choice into two parts. One part, solved by the budget line, is to describe the range of choice open to the consumer. The other part is to determine which combination of commodities, of all those on the budget line, the consumer will pick. The first part incorporates the basic economic data, and for it the economist assumes full responsibility. The second part depends on psychological data, and concerning it the economist can say only that the consumer will pick the combination on the budget line that he likes best. This apparently feeble response to the second part of the problem means that the budget line alone does not determine consumers' decisions; that more data are needed—data about preferences of consumers. We now set about introducing these data.

Suppose that last month Mrs. X had bought 50 pounds of vegetables and, therefore, 30 pounds of meat (point *A* on Fig. 5-2), and suppose that she had run short of meat before the end of the month. Then as she made this month's choice,

---

[1] If there were three commodities, the equation for the budget line would be (let us say) $p_1x + p_2y + p_3z = B$, where x, y, and z denote the quantities purchased of the three commodities. The extension of this concept to larger numbers of commodities is obvious.

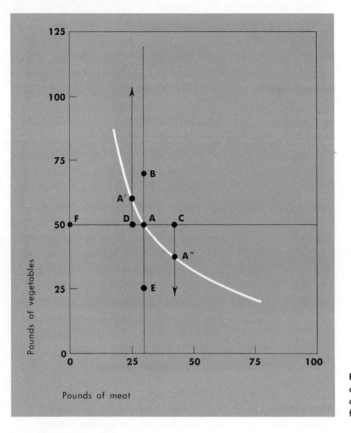

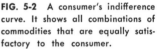

FIG. 5-2 A consumer's indifference curve. It shows all combinations of commodities that are equally satisfactory to the consumer.

she would judge market basket *A* to be less desirable than other combinations that include more meat, such as 45 pounds of vegetables and 32 of meat (which costs the same). In this way her tastes and experiences enable her to compare mentally the desirabilities of any pair of market baskets.

To the practical Mrs. X the contemplation of any combinations of amounts of vegetables and meat other than those she can afford would seem a waste of time. But let us disregard that practical consideration for a moment, and in fact think of comparisons among *all conceivable* market baskets of meat and vegetables. Then, taking market basket *A* as a point of departure, every other conceivable market basket will be a member of one of three classes: (1) the class of market baskets that are preferred to *A;* (2) the class of those that are inferior to *A;* and (3) the class that are as satisfactory as *A* (meaning, for this class, market baskets that Mrs. X deems to be about as desirable as market basket *A,* but no more desirable).

So much is empty classification. To give our reasoning substance, we must notice some prevalent characteristics of consumers' preferences.

In the first place, if a market basket has more of either commodity than *A* and no less of the other, it will be preferred to *A*. On this basis, market basket *B* (30 pounds meat, 70 pounds vegetables) would be preferred to *A* (30 pounds meat, 50 pounds vegetables), and so would market basket *C* (35 pounds meat, 50 pounds vegetables). In fact, any market basket that lies in the area to the north and east of *A* in Fig. 5-2 would be preferred to market basket *A*. By the same reasoning, market basket *D* (25 pounds meat, 50 pounds vegetables) is inferior to *A*. So is market basket E (30 pounds meat, 25 pounds vegetables) and, in general, any market basket southwest of A. (We cannot yet say anything about market baskets to the northwest or southeast of A.)

The assumption we have just made is known as the *postulate of nonsatiation*. It asserts that consumers normally prefer more to less—or, less tersely, that if a consumer can obtain more of one commodity without having to give up any of any other, he will do so.

Now let us return to market basket D, which contains less meat than A. Suppose we add a pound of vegetables to it, to obtain a market basket a slight distance up along the arrow drawn through D. The result will be a market basket that is preferred to D, by the nonsatiation postulate, and that may or may not be preferred to A. If this new market basket is still judged inferior to A (judged by Mrs. X, that is), add another pound of vegetables to it, thus moving to a basket farther up the arrow. It is reasonable to suppose that as we move up the arrow we shall eventually come to a market basket, say A', that Mrs. X would feel is as satisfactory as A.[2]

This reasoning has introduced a second assumption, called the *substitutability postulate*. This postulate holds that if a small amount of one commodity is subtracted from a market basket, the deficiency can be made good by an adequate increase in the amount (or amounts) of the other commodities. By virtue of the substitutability postulate there is a point on the upward arrow through market basket D which is just as satisfactory as market basket A. We have already called this point A'.

We can make a similar analysis for market basket C, which contains more meat than A and is therefore superior to it. This time, though, we shall have to move downward to find the point, called A'', at which our basket would contain 5 pounds more meat than A and just enough fewer vegetables so that it would be just as satisfactory as A.

There was clearly nothing special about points D and C. If we start with any market basket on the horizontal line through A (except one unduly close to F), we can move upward or downward as is appropriate (i.e., add or subtract vegetables) to find a point like A' or A'' that is as satisfactory as A. If we do this a large number of times, and string all those points together, they will form a curve like the curve drawn through A', A, A'', with the characteristic that any point on it represents a market basket that is as satisfactory as the market basket represented by point A. This curve is called the *indifference curve through A*. (It could as well be called the indifference curve through A'.)

An indifference curve consists of all points that represent market baskets which a consumer regards as equally satisfactory.

Clearly such an indifference curve can be drawn through any market basket represented in the diagram by drawing a horizontal line through it and following

[2] This is not inevitable, however. Suppose we start from F, the market basket with as much in the way of vegetables as A but with no meat at all. It is quite possible that no matter how many vegetables you load onto it, you will not get a market basket that Mrs. X would feel is as good as A; her family would rather have a skimpy diet with some meat than a lavish vegetarian menu.

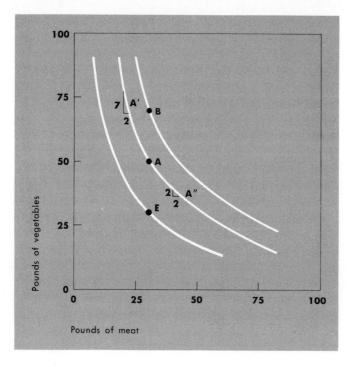

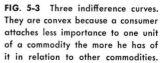

FIG. 5-3 Three indifference curves. They are convex because a consumer attaches less importance to one unit of a commodity the more he has of it in relation to other commodities.

the same reasoning. These indifference curves incorporate all the psychological data that are pertinent to the consumer's choice, just as the budget line incorporates all the relevant economic data. We must therefore point out a number of the characteristics of these curves.

Figure 5-3 shows three indifference curves, one through market basket *B,* one through *A,* and one through *E.* These curves are, in essence, a scale for ranking the desirabilities of the different market baskets. For example, basket *B* is superior to basket *A* (by the nonsatiation postulate); and any market basket on the curve through *B* is as satisfactory as *B* (by construction), and is therefore superior to any market basket on the curve through *A*—and, all the more, to any market basket on the curve through *E.* (It follows at once that the indifference curves cannot cross each other; draw a diagram in which two indifference curves *do* cross, and you'll see that you've violated the nonsatiation postulate.)

Notice in Fig. 5-3 that the indifference curves slope downward to the right (and recall, incidentally, that since *A'* has less meat than *A,* if it is rated as desirable as *A* it must have more vegetables). Note also that the indifference curves curl upward or, in mathematical language, are convex. This characteristic reflects a new psychological assumption. Suppose that 2 pounds of meat are taken out of market basket *A',* shown by the short horizontal line marked "2." Market basket *A'* did not contain very much meat to begin with, so a large offsetting increase in the amount of vegetables (marked "7") is needed to produce a market basket that has 2 pounds less meat than *A'* but is just as desirable. On the other hand, if basket *A",* which has a large allotment of meat, is taken as a point of departure, it seems reasonable that only a small increase in vegetables (also marked "2") is needed to compensate for a 2-pound reduction in the amount of meat. The psychological assumption that underlies this reasoning is called the *postulate of diminishing marginal substitutability.*

74

The postulate of diminishing marginal substitutability asserts that the more a market basket contains of one particular commodity in proportion to others, the smaller will be the increases in the amounts of other commodities needed to compensate psychologically for a unit decrease in the amount of that one.

There are many exceptions to this postulate, but it does express the quite usual fact that the more a consumer has of anything, the less importance he attaches to having one unit more or less of it.

Now we can bring together the psychological data contained in the indifference curves with the economic data contained in the budget line. See Fig. 5-4, where the budget line is shown together with four indifference curves labeled I, II, III, and IV. Mrs. X cannot afford any market basket on indifference curve I because it lies entirely above the budget line, which shows the greatest quantity of vegetables she can afford in conjunction with any given quantity of meat. But she can afford at least one market basket on each of the other indifference curves shown. She will choose a market basket on the highest indifference curve she can afford—namely, indifference curve II. Because of the shapes of the indifference curves, market basket C (26 pounds meat, 60 pounds vegetables) is the only combination on curve II that she can afford. Her decision is determined.

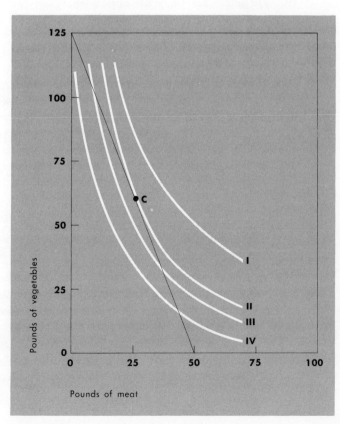

FIG. 5-4 The consumer's choice. Maximum satisfaction occurs where the budget line touches the highest attainable indifference curve.

Thus the problem of consumers' choice with given budget, prices, and tastes is solved—though one property of the solution deserves particular emphasis. Notice that the budget line is tangent to the indifference curve through the market basket chosen, market basket C. Because this is the only point on the budget line where this relationship holds, we can summarize our result by saying

> The consumer will choose the combination of goods at which the budget line is tangent to an indifference curve.

That's just geometry. To see the economic meaning of this condition, we must look into the significances of the slopes of the budget line and the indifference curve, which are equal at the point chosen.

SOME TECHNICAL CONCEPTS

The economic meaning of the slope of the budget line is elementary. Starting from any point on the line, if Mrs. X buys one less pound of meat she will save $1, with which she can buy 2½ pounds of vegetables. Therefore, the line climbs 2½ units every time it moves one unit to the left. In general terms, if the price of the commodity plotted horizontally is p_1 and that of the commodity plotted vertically is p_2, buying one unit less of the horizontal commodity will save p_1, with which p_1/p_2 units of the vertical commodity can be bought. The slope of the budget line will therefore be p_1/p_2, and depends entirely on the ratio of the prices.

The interpretation of the slope of the indifference curve at any point is almost as easy. Remember that in the small triangles drawn in Fig. 5-3 (which shows the quantity of vegetables needed to compensate for a small decrease in the amount of meat) two of the vertices of the triangle drawn at A' lie on the indifference curve through A'. The chord drawn through those two vertices is an approximation to the tangent at A', and the approximation will become better and better as we think of drawing smaller and smaller triangles. In fact, the tangent is the mathematical limit of those chords as the triangles diminish in size. But the slope of each such chord is the number of pounds of vegetables (the vertical leg) needed to compensate Mrs. X for relinquishing the number of pounds of meat represented by the horizontal leg, or the compensating number of pounds of vegetables per pound of meat foregone. This is a very important concept in economics, known as the *marginal rate of substitution* (abbreviated MRS).

> The marginal rate of substitution of any commodity Y for any other commodity Z is the number of units of Y needed per unit of Z to compensate the consumer for foregoing a small quantity of Z. It is represented graphically by the slope or tangent of an indifference curve.

For example, at point A' in Fig. 5-3, 7 pounds of vegetables are required to compensate Mrs. X for losing 2 pounds of meat. The MRS of vegetables for meat at that point is *approximately* 3.5.[3]

In short, the slope of the budget line shows the ratio at which the commodities can be exchanged for each other at the market prices, and the slope of the indifference curve shows the ratio at which the consumer would be just willing to

[3] We say "approximately" because the slope of the chord is only approximately the slope of the tangent.

exchange them for each other, i.e., the number of units of one that he could exchange for one unit of the other and be neither better nor worse off. At the market basket chosen, these two ratios are equal. So we conclude that:

> In allocating his budget between two commodities, the consumer will choose the market basket on his budget line for which the MRS between the two commodities is equal to the ratio of their prices.

In spite of the forest of technicalities, this is only common sense. Consider any point on Mrs. X's budget line for which the MRS of vegetables for meat is not 1: .40 = 2.5—say, a point at which it is 3.0. At that point 3 pounds of vegetables would be needed to compensate her for giving up one pound of meat, or one pound of meat is as desirable to her as 3 pounds of vegetables. But she can obtain an additional pound of meat by giving up only 2½ pounds of vegetables. If she found herself at such a point, she would move to a higher indifference curve by buying 2½ pounds fewer of vegetables and one pound more of meat, and she would continue to improve her position by moving southeast along her budget line until she reached the point where her MRS was equal to the price ratio.

The same is true for market baskets on the other side of the optimal point. At a point where the MRS is 2.0, 2 pounds of vegetables would be as valuable in her esteem as one pound of meat. But she can obtain 2½ pounds of vegetables by reducing her purchase of meat by one pound and, again, she would not choose such a point. The only point at which she cannot improve her position by reallocating her purchases is the one at which her MRS is equal to the ratio of the prices.

Still another way to express the same conclusion is to say:

> In allocating his budget between two commodities the consumer will choose the market basket on his budget line at which an additional dollar's worth of one commodity is just as desirable as an additional dollar's worth of the other.

This conclusion says exactly the same thing as went before, but in simpler language: we can expect the consumer to shift his dollars from one commodity to the other as long as he can increase his satisfaction by doing so—unless he is at the point where he is indifferent between additional dollar's worth of the two commodities. This is the same as our earlier conclusion (that a dollar's worth of one commodity would be deemed just as desirable as a dollar's worth of the other), because if we measure quantities in dollars' worth rather than in pounds, the price ratio is by definition 1:1, and we have asserted that in that case the MRS for the market basket chosen must be 1:1.

If the upshot, then, can be reduced to such commonsense, self-evident terms, why all the folderol about indifference curves, marginal rates of substitution, and all that? There are two reasons. First, we have been forced to make explicit many of the assumptions that lie hidden behind commonsense reasoning, and so have a better idea of when it is applicable and when not.[4] Second, we have laid a foundation

---

[4] Just to indicate how easy it is to slip assumptions in unnoticed, here are some others that were used implicitly in our reasoning. (1) *Completeness:* that the consumer can compare any two bundles and decide which is preferable or whether they are equally satisfactory. He never "just doesn't know which he prefers." (2) *Transitivity:* that if *A, B,* and *C* are three bundles of goods, any consumer who prefers *A* to *B* and *B* to *C* also prefers *A* to *C.* This is an

for the analysis of consumers' responses to changes in the size of their budgets or in the prices of the things they buy.

We have now answered our preliminary question: How will a consumer with a given amount of money to spend divide his purchases among different goods so as to obtain maximum satisfaction? But the answer—to equate his MRS to the ratio of the prices—was derived from an example using only two goods: meat and vegetables. Now we must do three things. (1) We must extend this answer to the more realistic case where numerous goods are involved. (2) We must ask how the consumer's spending will be affected if the amount of income at his disposal is changed. (3) We must ask how his purchases will be affected if the relative prices of different goods change. (This last question, indeed, will lead us to a central objective of this chapter—namely, the derivation of demand curves.) We shall take up each of these matters in turn, and all our reasoning will depend on the logical apparatus we have developed to answer the preliminary question.

More than Two Commodities

Of course, neither our Mrs. X nor any other consumer normally is concerned with a choice between just two commodities. The importance of the foregoing analysis lies in the fact that the concepts there expounded are applicable no matter how many commodities are involved in the consumer's decision. If a budget is to be allocated among any number of commodities, there is a budget line determined by the total budget and the prices of all the commodities. Preferences among market baskets can be described by indifference curves, no matter how many different commodities are represented in each market basket. There is a marginal rate of substitution between every pair of commodities in a market basket and, when a sensible selection has been made, the MRS for every pair must be equal to the ratio of their prices. All this is just as in the two-commodity case, but the argument behind these assertions cannot be reduced to a problem in plane geometry when more than two commodities are involved. Since the argument requires new technicalities but no essential new ideas, however, we shall omit it.

Response to Changes in the Budget

Thus far we have seen how a consumer permitted to spend a given budget divides it among commodities at given prices. It is at least as important to economic analysis to see how consumers respond to changes in these data, to which we now advance.

The amount that a consumer spends on any commodity depends on the total amount of money that he is permitted to spend: his budget. When consumers' incomes change, causing changes in their consumption budgets, their demand curves for commodities shift, with important impacts on commodity markets. Consumers in advanced, wealthy countries divide their budgets quite differently from con-

---

obvious prerequisite to making consistent decisions. (3) *Continuity:* that if bundle *A* is preferred to bundle B we can take away a very small quantity of any commodity from bundle *A* and have left a bundle that will still be preferred to bundle *B*. This disallows the preferences of a drunkard, for example, who might prefer a quart of whiskey and a small hamburger to 31 ounces of whiskey and the most delicious dinner conceivable.

For a somewhat more rigorous treatment of consumption theory see our companion volume, *The Price System,* in this Series. For a still fuller discussion see Peter Newman, *The Theory of Exchange* (Englewood Cliffs, N.J.: Prentice-Hall, 1965), or any other good intermediate text on economic theory.

sumers in poor, underdeveloped countries. Expenditure patterns are not the same in prosperous times as during depressions. These are the phenomena that the theory of the present section illuminates.

We can regard any single purchase decision as a choice between just two commodities. This may seem surprising, when there are so many commodities in the world, but let us look closely at a purchase decision and see what the issues are. Suppose that Mrs. X, our typical consumer, has $50 to spend on all foods, including meat, and that she is now standing before the meat counter. The issue that confronts her is simply that the more she spends on meat, the less she will have left over for everything else on her shopping list. She confronts, at that moment, a two-commodity problem, the two commodities being meat and money left over for other things (MLO for short). This choice can be represented on the now-familiar two-commodity diagram, remembering that, by definition, MLO is $1 per unit.

Taking this point of view, the two-commodity diagram makes it easy to represent the effect of changes in Mrs. X's budgetary allowance on her purchases of meat. Let x stand for the number of pounds of meat purchased, y for the amount of MLO, and B for Mrs. X's total budget. Then, since the prices of a pound of meat and of a unit of MLO both happen to be $1, Mrs. X's budgetary constraint or budget line is

$$x + y = B.$$

This line is shown in Figure 5-5 for three levels of B—$40, $50, and $60. Note that the three budget lines are parallel to each other, because the slope of the line depends on the ratio of the prices of the two "commodities," and not at all on the amount of money available for expenditure.[5] In terms of the diagram, a change in the amount available for expenditure shifts the budget line vertically up and down, and has no other effect on it.

Mrs. X's psychological preferences are expressed by indifference curves in which the appropriate commodities now are meat and MLO. To be sure, MLO is an artificial or composite commodity. The desirability of y of MLO is simply the desirability of the best combination of foods other than meat that Mrs. X could buy with $y. But this does not affect our reasoning, and there exist indifference curves between MLO and meat just as between vegetables and meat.

Whatever may be the value of B, Mrs. X will select the point on the corresponding budget line at which it touches the highest accessible indifference curve. (Three indifference curves and the consumption choices that they determine are shown in the figure.) When Mrs. X has $40 to spend on food she buys 21¼ pounds of meat; when she has $50 she buys 25 pounds; when she has $60, 29 pounds. We can think of drawing budget lines for other budgetary limits (e.g., $45) and of determining the corresponding purchases of meat. Finally, we can think of connecting by a line all the points so determined. This line, called Mrs. X's *expansion path* for meat purchases, is drawn in the figure. It shows how her purchases of meat are influenced by changes in the budget available to her.

As drawn, the expansion path has a slight downward curvature. This shape is

[5] If meat were to cost $1.25 a pound, the equation of the budget lines would be $1.25 X + Y = B$ and the slope of the budget lines would be different from the one shown. But, for the moment, we are not assuming this to be the case.

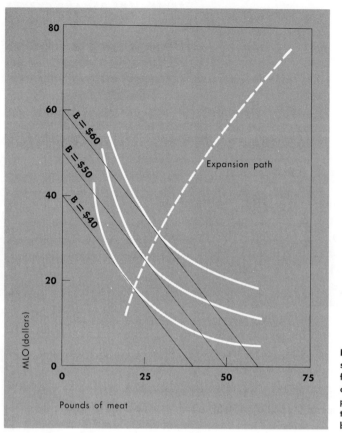

FIG. 5-5 Effects of different consumption budgets. The budget lines for different levels of expenditure are parallel to each other. The expansion path connects the points that will be chosen on different budget lines.

characteristic of the expansion paths for luxury goods because it indicates that out of every successive $1 increment in budget a slightly larger proportion will be spent on meat than was spent from the previous increment.[6] The expansion path for a necessity would curl upward because as a consumer's budget is increased gradually the proportion of each successive increase spent on necessities diminishes. It is even possible for the expansion path to turn back on itself—that is, although it must start out (for very low incomes) pointing generally northeast, it may curve upwards until eventually it points northwest. This would indicate that actually less of the commodity in question is purchased at high incomes than at some lower ones. These commodities are known as *inferior goods.* Familiar examples are cheap grades of clothing, poorer cuts of meat, visits to lower-class resort areas.

Figure 5-5 shows how a consumer's tastes, described by his indifference curves, determine the amount of a commodity that he purchases at different levels of consumption expenditure. Since the total budget is not one of the axes in this diagram, however, the actual relationship between it and purchases of a specific commodity is shown more clearly by another type of graph, known as an *Engel curve.* The Engel curve corresponding to Fig. 5-5 is shown in Figure 5-6. The total budget is there plotted horizontally, and the amount of meat purchased is plotted vertically. For example, a purchase of 21¼ pounds of meat is shown cor-

[6] Check this for yourself: If the expansion path became horizontal, the entire increment in income would be spent on meat.

responding to a food budget of $40. Figure 5-7 shows empirical Engel curves, based on a survey of American consumption habits. The curve for food consumed at home displays the shape characteristic of necessities; the curve for meals eaten out is typical of purchases of luxuries.

Responses to Price Changes; Demand Curves

Common sense leads us to conclude that when the price of a commodity rises consumers use less of it, and when it falls they use more. Like most commonsense conclusions, this one is usually true, but not always. The concepts that we have been developing permit us to gain a deeper insight as to why.

Figure 5-8 shows again Mrs. X's indifference curves for meat and MLO. Three budget lines are shown, all corresponding to a total expenditure, of $50 on food. The one labeled "$p = \$1$" is already familiar; it is the one that applies when meat costs $1 a pound, and corresponds to the formula

$$x + y = 50.$$

The higher line applies when the price of meat is 75¢ a pound; its formula is

$$.75x + y = 50.$$

The lower line applies when meat costs $1.25 a pound. (What is its formula?) Note that these three budget lines form a cone emanating from the point for no meat, $50 MLO. The other ends of the lines show how much meat can be purchased

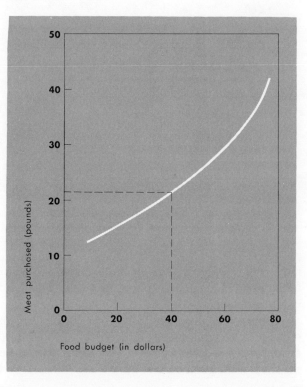

FIG. 5-6 An Engel curve. Consumption of this commodity is higher for higher consumption budgets.

Food budget (in dollars)

Meat purchased (pounds)

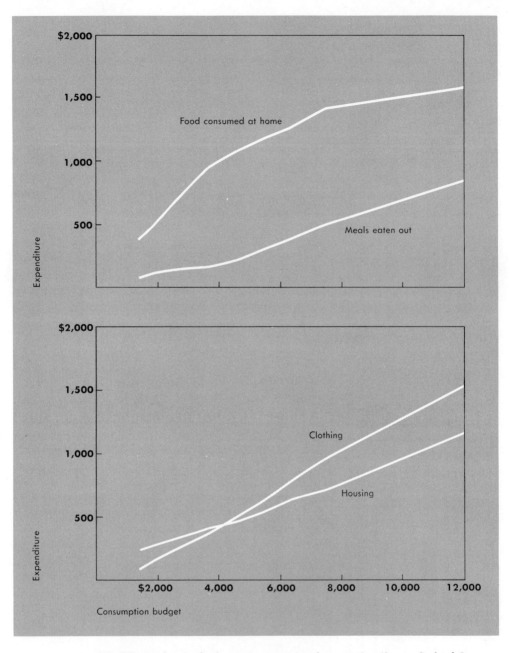

FIG. 5-7   Engel curves for four major categories of consumption. (Source: *Study of Consumer Expenditures, Incomes, and Savings,* University of Pennsylvania Press, 1957.

if the entire budget is spent on that commodity. The geometric effect of an increase in the price of meat is simply to make the budget line steeper, rotating it around its left endpoint.

When Mrs. X stands at the meat counter she makes her decision in the light of the price of meat, among other things. To each price of meat there corresponds, as we have just seen, a budget line, and (without thinking of graphs, of course) she chooses the point on that budget line where it just touches the highest accessible

82

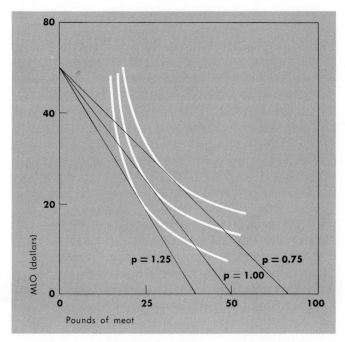

FIG. 5-8 Effect of a price change. A change in the price of a commodity changes the slope of the budget lines. The effect on purchases is shown by the points of tangency between indifference curves and budget lines, though not very clearly.

indifference curve. The indifference curves and decision points corresponding to three prices of meat are shown in the figure. Mrs. X's decisions accord with our expectations: at a price of $1.25 per pound she buys 23 pounds; at $1 a pound she buys 25 pounds; at 75¢ a pound she buys 29 pounds.[7]

An increase in the price of a commodity has two effects on a consumer: the *income effect* and the *substitution effect*. The income effect is illustrated by the fact that the higher prices of meat, corresponding to the steeper budget lines, force Mrs. X down to lower indifference curves, just as a reduction in her budgetary allowance would. In a real sense they impoverish her. We already know that, inferior goods apart, a reduction in the budget induces a reduction in consumption of a commodity. The substitution effect arises directly from the increasing steepness of the budget line as the price increases. We also already know that this consumer will choose the point on her budget line where the MRS of MLO for meat is equal to the price of meat (the price of MLO being always 1). If the price of meat rises, the MRS of MLO for meat at the choice point must rise, too. But the MRS rises as we move to the left along an indifference curve or budget line, i.e., in the direction of buying less meat. Thus, normally, an increase in the price of a commodity induces a decrease in purchases of it in two ways: first, by forcing the typical consumer to a lower indifference curve; and second, by inducing the consumer to substitute other things for it, as indicated by a movement to the left along the highest indifference curve that can be reached.[8]

[7] This result is not, however, inevitable: you can easily draw indifference curves according to which Mrs. X will buy less meat ·at 75¢ a pound than at $1 a pound. Of course, they will represent *different* tastes, but they will represent *possible* tastes.

[8] In the case of an inferior good, the first effect (the income effect) of the increase in price will tend to increase consumption of the good, and in extreme instances this will outweigh the second (the substitution) effect. This is how an increase in price can lead to an increase in purchases. The good in question, however must be both an inferior good, and such an important item of consumption that the income effect is substantial.

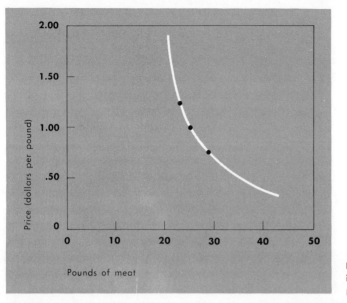

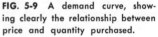

FIG. 5-9 A demand curve, showing clearly the relationship between
price and quantity purchased.

The relationship between price and the amount purchased is not shown very clearly in Fig. 5-8 because the price is indicated there only by the slope of the budget line. But the same data can be displayed, as in Figure 5-9, by plotting prices vertically and showing for each price the quantity that Mrs. X will purchase at that price. For example, Fig. 5-8 shows that Mrs. X will choose 23 pounds of meat when the price is $1.25 a pound; this datum is shown on Fig. 5-9 by the highest of the three emphasized points. The budget line for $1 a pound on Fig. 5-8 shows that Mrs. X will buy 25 pounds at that price. This information is transcribed onto Fig. 5-9 and is represented by the middle emphasized point. In this way, each possible budget line on Fig. 5-8 gives rise to a single point on Fig. 5-9, the point which shows how much meat Mrs. X will buy at the price corresponding to that budget line. When all these points are strung together, the result is Mrs. X's demand curve for meat. It shows vividly how the quantity she buys diminishes as the price increases, and summarizes both the economic and the psychological data that determine her decisions at different possible prices.

MARKET DEMAND CURVES

So much for Mrs. X. We have analyzed her purchasing decisions in some detail, but they are not of much practical importance except to her immediate family. What is important is that Mrs. Y, Mrs. Z, and all the other ladies who buy meat (and shoes, and sealing wax) have indifference curves too, from which their individual demand curves can be determined. These individual demand curves add up to a market demand curve just as, on the other side, the supply curves of individual firms add up to a market supply curve. For example, we know that at $1.25 a pound Mrs. X (who has proved too valuable an example to forget) will buy 23 pounds of meat. Suppose that Mrs. Y, whose husband avoids potatoes, will buy 25 pounds (of meat) at that price, and that Mrs. Z, confined by a more stringent budget, will buy but 22 pounds, and that somehow these three constitute the entire market. Then the market demand at a price of $1.25 will be 70 pounds. In the same way, at a price of $1 a pound, Mrs. X will buy 25 pounds of meat. If Mrs. Y then buys 26 pounds and Mrs. Z 24 pounds, the total market demand will be 75 pounds at a price of $1 a pound. Continuing thus, we can ascertain the market demand at every possible price simply by adding up the demands of individual consumers at that price. The result, when graphed, is the market demand curve that we set out to explain.

Now the time has come to look at a real demand curve. It is manifestly impractical to build up the demand curve for a commodity by duplicating our conceptual procedure—that is, by ascertaining the budgets and indifference maps of individual consumers and working from there out. In actual practice, one obtains records on the past behavior of the market (the prices charged, the quantities sold, and other data) and infers from them, by a fairly elaborate statistical analysis, what the demand curve must be.

Figure 5-10 is about as close as we can come to a genuine demand curve without elaborate processing of the data. It shows data on the price and consumption of electric power for domestic use in 53 widely-scattered American communities. Each dot shows the data for a single community. For example, the dot

FIG. 5-10 Demand curve for electric power. Even in the case of such a cheap necessity as electric power, consumers tend to use less when the price is high. (Source: Reports of the Federal Power Commission.)

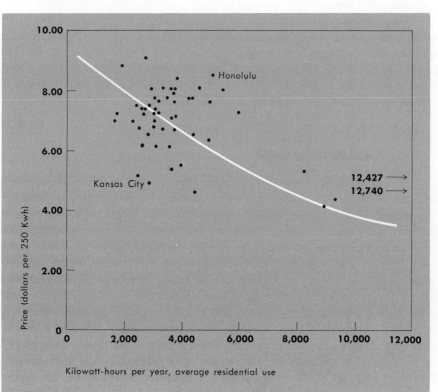

labeled "Honolulu" shows that in that city the typical cost for consuming 250 kilowatt-hours ("kwh" for short) in a month is $8.52, and that the typical household there consumes 5,084 kwh a year. Each of the other dots shows the cost of electric power, and the average annual usage by a household, for a different community.

The general appearance is far different from the smooth and regular progression of an idealized curve, such as in Fig. 5-9. Of course it is. Any family's use of electric power is influenced by many factors in addition to power rates: the family's income, the number of children, the size of the house, the output of electrical appliances, the prices of competing products such as gas, the climate of the city, and many more. These other factors are so important that we are hardly aware that the price of electric current makes any difference at all to our decisions. Accordingly, the average use of electric power in a city is affected by the proportion of families in each income bracket, the proportion of families of different sizes, the proportions living in houses and apartments of different sizes, the climate, the price of household gas, and many other conditions in addition to the price of electricity. No wonder these dots scatter all over, and no wonder that a good deal of statistical adjustment, to allow for these other factors, is required to bring out clearly the effect of differences in the price of power. Nevertheless, it is evident in this figure that these complicating factors tend to average out, and that there is a general tendency to use more power where it is cheaper. Neither city where the price of 250 kwh was in the neighborhood of $9 used as much as 3,000 kwh per household per year. One city where the price was under $5 used less than 4,000 kwh per year, but that one turns out to be Kansas City, Kansas, where natural gas is exceptionally cheap.

This general tendency to use more power where the price is lower is shown by the curve drawn through the cloud of dots. It shows that *on the average,* consumption falls by about 385 kwh per year for every 1 mill increase in the price of a kwh. Though that is what our theory leads us to expect, it is still a little surprising to see it borne out in the case of a commodity for which the price appears to be such an insignificant element in the purchase decision.

"A GRAIN OF SALT"

The adage "Custom is stronger than reason" applies just as surely to purchase decisions as it does to any other decision. No housewife out shopping can be constantly cudgeling her brain with questions like "Does my family need these shoelaces more than any other 25¢ item I can think of?" Many families, following long-standing customs, eat fish on Friday but meat the rest of the week, and have Sunday dinner out—and few review this pattern every week in the light of the current prices of fish, meat, and restaurant meals. Yet these customary purchase patterns are not impervious to price changes: the family that eats out pays attention to the right-hand side of the menu, and the fish-once-a-week housewife may respond to a swordfish sale on Tuesday. More fundamentally, though, if prices rise or the pay envelope falls until the customary pattern of purchases costs more than the household can afford, the pattern *has* to be changed. And that change will (the great majority of the time, at least) consist in skimping on the items that provide least satisfaction per dollar to the family.

The theory of consumption sketched in this chapter can best be thought of as a theory of how customary patterns of consumption are formed and altered in the light of how much different things cost and how much the family can afford. To be sure, throughout the chapter we talked of individual purchase decisions, but that was only for simplicity. For our purposes the individual purchase is much less important than the family's general purchase policy. Our concern is not with the amount of meat that Mrs. X will buy next Tuesday, but rather with the amount she will buy on the average—week in and week out at different levels of meat prices and other data. If our theory is understood in this light, as a description of the kinds of purchase policy that are evolved in the light of experience and stand the test of time, then it may not appear to be such an unrealistic caricature as it seems when taken literally. In this spirit, then, let us evaluate the main conclusions of the chapter.

A typical consumer or family has a limited budget to divide among all the different goods and services it wants and needs. This is not, as we assumed in the text, a precise number (e.g., $50 a week for meat and vegetables); rather, it is a general appreciation, acquired through experience, of what the family can afford to spend in the light of its income, its obligations, its expectations, and its habits of saving. Just as the family learns what it can afford to spend by observing the general drift of its assets and debts, so it learns how to divide its budget among different commodities by experience and incessant experimentation. If the payments on the old car were met without trouble, the family is likely to think of a fancier car when the time comes for replacement. If the budget pinches, the family is likely to make a choice between Friday night at the movies and Sunday dinner out, or may make its old bowling shoes last a little longer, or find some other means of retrenchment. In short, while most purchases are an unthinking repetition of habitual patterns, the family is constantly probing for possible changes in these patterns, shifting expenditures from one commodity to another to see whether it can obtain more satisfaction from its expenditures (technically, to see whether it can reach a higher indifference curve).

In reality this probing never stops, but our analysis has shown the nature of the purchase pattern that is being sought: it is the purchase pattern in which the transfer of a dollar from any commodity to any other will neither increase the family's satisfaction appreciably, nor diminish it. In technical language, the pattern sought is one wherein the marginal rate of substitution between any pair of commodities is in the same ratio as their prices. Though this exact pattern is not likely ever to be attained, obvious discrepancies from it are soon corrected, and the family's actual pattern is normally not far different from this ideal one.

A few implications follow immediately. If a product's price rises, a dollar spent on it will no longer buy as much satisfaction as before. The pattern of expenditures that was ideal before the price change will no longer be appropriate, and families will migrate toward new consumption patterns in which less of this commodity is used. This is the logic behind the demand curves. On the other hand, if a family's income rises, the pressure restraining the consumption of all commodities will be relaxed. The family will be able to afford a higher indifference curve and indeed will move toward one, still maintaining the same marginal rates of substitution between every pair of commodities. This is the logic behind the Engel curves.

IMPLICATIONS OF THE ANALYSIS

We have found that there is an essential logic to consumers' decisions and their consumption patterns, even when our theorizing is taken with the recommended grain of salt. It is by virtue of this logic that consumers' decisions are significant for the economy. In fact, consumers' decisions are the ultimate guides of economic activity, a condition known as *consumers' sovereignty*. Let us see how it works.

We have found that a typical consumer, like our unforgettable Mrs. X, will divide a budget among commodities so that an additional dollar's worth of any one commodity is as desirable as an additional dollar's worth of any other. Suppose, for example, that after Mrs. X had decided on her best consumption bundle (point *C* of Fig. 5-4) she discovered an additional $1 in her purse. Then it would be practically a matter of indifference whether she spent it to buy one pound of meat or 2½ pounds of vegetables.

Since all consumers trade at the same prices (more or less) the same is true of Mrs. Y, Mrs. Z, and everybody else. So we can say that the whole community is about equally desirous to have an additional pound of meat as to have 2½ additional pounds of vegetables. This is important information for farmers, for businessmen, and for anyone else concerned with arranging the productive efforts of the community. It informs them that if there is an opportunity anywhere for redirecting the use of land and other economic resources so as to increase the production of meat by more than a pound at a sacrifice of no more than 2½ pounds of vegetables, that opportunity ought to be taken. Similarly, if the output of vegetables can be increased by more than 2½ pounds by diverting resources that are being used to produce no more than one pound of meat, that ought to be done. In short, when all consumers face the same prices, those prices indicate the community's relative desires for the different commodities.

An economy is said to display consumer sovereignty when its productive activities are responsive to consumers' preferences as reflected in their purchasing choices.

We can already see, in a general way, that consumers will be sovereign in an economy in which consumers and producers make their decisions in the light of prices, and all use the same prices. For suppose that some farmer can convert a field from pasture to a vegetable plot, reducing his output of meat by 300 pounds and increasing his output of vegetables by 900 pounds. Then, if the prices for which he sells meat and vegetables are the same as those at which Mrs. X buys, his sales of meat will fall by $300, his sales of vegetables will rise by $360, and he will enjoy a net increase of $60 in the value of his output. Then he will convert the land to vegetable production and, indeed, will divide his efforts between meat and vegetable-raising so that further increases in vegetable output cost him .4 pounds of meat for each pound of vegetables produced.

Of course, the farmer's wholesale prices are not the same as Mrs. X's retail prices, and the story is more complicated than this. But we already know the essence of it. We acquired the key in our study of production, where we found that under competitive conditions, businessmen will arrange production so that the marginal costs of producing every pair of commodities are proportional to their prices. This means that if some resources are transferred from producing one commodity to another, the decline in output of the commodity that is cut back will have the same money value (and, we now see, the same psychological value) to consumers as the increase in output of the commodity that is expanded. In other words, under competitive conditions, commodities are produced in the proportions that consumers want. A competitive economy obeys consumers' sovereignty.

There is one implication of this analysis that helps tie all its loose threads together. Suppose that there is a general inflation in which the prices of all commodities rise in the same proportion, and suppose that there is some family whose earnings also rise in that proportion. Since the ratios of the prices of different commodities will not change, neither will the marginal rates of substitution among commodities. Since the family will be able to afford, and just afford, the pre-inflation level of consumption of all commodities (its income having risen in the same proportion as the cost of that expenditure pattern), it is neither tempted nor compelled to change its consumption pattern for financial reasons. In this highly unlikely situation, therefore, the family will continue to consume just what it did before the inflation.

Table 5-1 EXAMPLE OF THE EFFECT OF UNIVERSAL INFLATION ON CONSUMERS' BUDGETS

Commodity	Weekly Consumption	Before Inflation		After Inflation	
		Price	Cost	Price	Cost
Meat	16 pounds	$1.00	$16.00	$1.10	$17.60
Fruit juice	20 pints	.30	6.00	.33	6.60
Bowling	8 strings	.40	3.20	.44	3.52
Expenditure	—	—	25.20	—	27.72
Income	—	—	28.00	—	30.80

An example will make this clearer. Table 5-1 presents data for a family with an income, before inflation, of $28.00 a week, 10 per cent of which it saves, and 90 per cent of which it spends on the three commodities listed, which are all that it consumes. Its pre-inflation pattern of consumption is shown in the second column. Note that these quantities account for exactly 90 per cent of its income. Note also that at those consumption levels one string of bowling is deemed to be worth just as much as the 1⅓ pints of fruit juice, or the .4 pounds of meat that 40¢ will buy. After the inflation, the family's income and spendable budget have both risen by 10 per cent, but so have all prices. Therefore, the pre-inflation pattern of consumption will just absorb the amount of income available for consumption. And, since one string of bowling will still be exchangeable for 1⅓ pints of fruit juice (and so forth), there is nothing to be gained by altering the pattern of expenditure. The price changes and the income change cancel each other out.

The importance of this remark is twofold. First, it shows that price changes (especially if they are widespread) and income changes are very much the same kind of thing. Every trade-union leader appreciates this; he knows that as far as his members are concerned, an increase in the consumers' price index is the same thing as a cut in their wage rate. Second, this remark shows that the significant characteristic of a price system is the scheme of relative prices—the ratios of the prices of different commodities. The absolute prices are subsidiary; they are only a convenient vehicle for expressing the relative values of different commodities. (The statement that hamburger costs $1.35 a pound tells nothing to a person who doesn't know the prices of other commodities. Samuel Johnson understood this: when he was told that in the Hebrides one could buy an egg for a farthing, he said "That doesn't prove that eggs are cheap there, but only that money is hard to come by.") In brief:

The price system is a system of relative values of different commodities.

In a whole community of consumers, each allocating his budget so that the relative desirability of commodities is in the same proportion as their prices, these price ratios measure the relative desirability (per unit) of commodities to the community as a whole. This is the essential social message conveyed by prices. It tells how the community's resources should be allocated among the production of different commodities. If consumers are willing to pay as much for a pound of meat as for 3 pints of fruit juice, and if the resources required to produce 2 pints of the juice could produce a pound of meat, then consumers could be made better off if the resources were redirected from juice to meat production. Retail prices convey the desirability side of this comparison. Relative production costs, as we saw in earlier chapters, convey the information about the consequences of redirecting resources. The price system as a whole conveys all this information, as well as the motivation for acting on it, and that is why it is an almost indispensable tool for organizing production in a complicated economy. This is a theme to which we shall return often in this book.

SUMMARY

The main object of the theory of consumption is to explain demand curves, for it is through these that consumers' wants enter into the determination of prices, influence the amounts of different commodities that are produced and supplied, and ultimately contribute to the guidance of the economy.

The significance of a demand curve is derived from the logic of the consumers' decisions that stand behind it—logic revealed most clearly when a consumer has to divide a fixed budget between two commodities. Then the amount of the budget, together with the prices of the commodities, determines a budget line, a line that specifies all combinations of quantities of the two commodities that cost as much as the budget permits. The budget line incorporates all the objective data that influence the consumer's choice.

The subjective data, the consumer's needs and tastes, can be depicted by a set of indifference curves. Each indifference curve shows all combinations of quantities of the commodities that are just as satisfactory as each other. Every possible combination of commodities lies on some indifference curve; in general, if one combination contains more of one commodity than another, and no less of the second, it will be preferred and will lie on a "higher" indifference curve.

The indifference curves, together with the budget line, determine the consumer's choice: he will choose the combination on his budget line where it touches the highest possible indifference curve. The essential psychological properties of the combination chosen can be expressed in a number of different ways. One is to say that when the consumer has that combination, an additional dollar's worth of any commodity is deemed to be just as desirable as an additional dollar's worth of any other. A second way is to use the concept of the marginal rate of substitution: the marginal rate of substitution between any two commodities is the number of units of the first that would just compensate the consumer for the loss of one unit of the second. Graphically, the marginal rate of substitution at any point is the slope of the indifference curve through that point. In terms of this concept, the consumer chooses the point on his budget line at which the marginal rate of substitution between any two commodities is equal to the ratio of their prices.

A change in a consumers' income will result in a change in his consumption budget. Diagrammatically, this is represented by a parallel shift in his budget line. This permits the consumer's response to changes in his budget to be ascertained easily from his indifference-curve diagram. The amounts he consumes of a commodity, plotted against possible budgetary levels, are shown by his Engel curve for that commodity. Engel curves for necessities curl downward, curves for luxuries curl upward, and curves for inferior goods fall when the budget becomes large.

Demand curves also are derived conceptually from indifference-curve diagrams. For this purpose it is convenient to use a diagram in which the purchases of one commodity are shown horizontally and the amount of money left over for other things, MLO, is shown vertically. Then an increase in the price of the commodity is represented by a steepening of the budget line. This type of diagram shows that a price increase has a twofold effect. First, it makes the consumer poorer; he can no longer purchase the previous market basket unless his budget is increased. Second, if his budget is increased so that he can afford the old market basket, he will not want it. This will be so because the price is no longer equal to the marginal rate of substitution of MLO for the commodity when the old market basket is bought. In normal cases these two effects operate in the same direction: the consumer buys less of the commodity whose price has risen. He does this both because he is poorer and because, at the higher price, he prefers a combination where the marginal rate of substitution of MLO for the commodity is higher. Pathological cases aside, therefore, the consumer buys less of a commodity the higher its price, as is shown by the usual demand curve.

Since all consumers purchase at the same (or at least similar) prices, all consumers will have the same marginal rate of substitution between every pair of commodities. We are therefore justified in saying that there is a community marginal rate of substitution between every pair of commodities, and that it is equal to the ratio of their prices. But in our study of production we found that competitive businessmen tend to allocate productive resources in such a way that the ratio of the marginal costs of producing every pair of commodities is also equal to the ratio of their prices. Putting these facts together, we see that in competitive equilibrium every productive resource is being used in such a way that if it were shifted to a different commodity it would not produce goods that consumers valued more highly than the ones it currently produces; every resource is being used as consumers want it to be. An economic system that allocates resources in this way is said to obey consumers' sovereignty.

Monopoly and Oligopoly

CHAPTER SIX

In this chapter we shall descend somewhat from the high plane of generality and abstraction that we have been inhabiting. Thus far we have studied the behavior of competitive markets and their participants. Competitive markets are the simplest to understand, the most predictable, and the most conducive to efficient economic performance, and for these reasons hold a central place in economic analysis. But they are not the only kind of market or even, in modern industrial economies, the most prevalent. To understand the operation of real economies, we must therefore study the behavior of other types of market, too.

THE GENESIS
OF MONOPOLY AND OLIGOPOLY

The hallmark of a competitive market is that every participant in it is a price-taker. That is, everyone in it takes it for granted that he cannot affect the prices at which he buys or sells, so does the best he can in the light of those prices. For this situation to hold there must be a large number of suppliers in the market, tolerably equal in size, so that no one firm can have an appreciable effect on the price or aggregate supply of the commodity, and so that no one firm's actions significantly influence the fortunes of any other firm. It must also be true that consumers do not care much, if at all, which firm they buy from, so that they respond readily to small differences in the prices charged by different firms if any should arise. Some examples of competitive markets are women's clothing in manufacturing, coal in mining, and wheat in agriculture. In all those industries the firms are numerous and small, and the products of one firm are virtually indistinguishable from those of any other.

But modern methods of mass production and mass marketing tend to be incompatible with competition,[1] and it is easy to see why this is so. Consider, first, modern methods of production. They tend to require large amounts of fixed capital equipment, and to be characterized by *decreasing long-run costs*. That is to say, a large plant operating at an efficient volume of output will have lower average costs than a small plant operating at its most efficient level of output.

When these technological conditions obtain, even an industry that starts out competitive will soon degenerate into some other market form, because the firms in it will tend to grow in order to reduce their costs of production by operating larger, more efficient plants. But they will not all grow synchronously. Historical accidents will guarantee that some of the firms will build large, modern plants before the others, and these will be under strong pressure to cut their prices in order to attain sales volumes at which the large plants can operate efficiently and cover their enhanced fixed cost. Furthermore, by virtue of their increased efficiency, the large firms will be able to operate profitably at prices *below* the average costs of their smaller competitors. This will produce an unstable situation. One by one, the smaller firms will be driven out of the market, forced to bequeath their erstwhile customers to the larger firms—which therefore will grow larger still. Eventually only a few firms will remain, all of them large enough to reap the full advantages of economies of scale.

When this state of affairs is reached, true competition cannot survive. The exact outcome depends on many factors, including especially the proportion of the market that is served by a firm large enough to be fully efficient. In Chapter 3 (Table 3-2) we saw that frequently there is room for only two or three fully efficient firms, even in a large national market. Now, General Electric and Westinghouse cannot pretend that they are participants in a competitive market; both know that between the two of them they control the price and volume of ouput of many of the products they sell, and this knowledge cannot help but affect their behavior. They constitute an oligopoly (see Chapter 2). To repeat our definition:

> An oligopoly is a market in which there are a few firms, each of which recognizes that its actions have a significant impact on the price and supply of the commodity.

The process of consolidation that we have just described can go even further if economies of scale continue to accrue (i.e., if the long-run average-cost curve continues to decline), until a single firm is so large that it supplies the entire market,

---

[1] There is an unfortunate divergence between the technical meaning of the word "competition" and common usage. Participants in competitive markets do not "compete" with each other in the common meaning of the term; they merely respond to impersonal market forces. Participants in markets of other forms often do "compete" vigorously (each firm keeps a sharp eye on its rivals' prices and products, makes sure that its own prices are in line, and strives to offer a product with more sales appeal that the rival goods have), but they are not competitive according to the technical meaning of the word, which is reserved strictly for price competition. We, of course, shall always use the words "competition" and "competitive" in their technical senses, but shall have to use the verb "compete" in both meanings, for there is no adequate synonym. These things understood, there is not much risk of confusion.

or at least the great bulk of it. In that case only one firm will remain, and a monopoly will be established.

A monopoly is a market in which all or virtually all of the commodity is provided by a single seller.

Besides, as we shall see, oligopolists have strong incentives to merge their firms into a monopoly, which from their point of view is the more profitable market form. This is the origin of the trust-building movement of the late nineteenth century.[2] Trusts and other forms of monopoly are now illegal in this country and most others, except in special circumstances. Nevertheless, the eternal vigilance of the Anti-Trust Division of the Department of Justice is required to prevent monopolies from re-emerging in various surreptitious forms.

An extreme form of economies of scale is a so-called *natural monopoly,* exemplified by local electric power companies, telephone companies, and other public utilities. There the technical advantages of supply by one large firm are so commanding that a single firm is licensed by the government to serve the entire market. In return for this exclusive license, or franchise, the firm submits to control by regulatory authorities which endeavor to assure adequate service at reasonable prices on the part of firms that are insulated from any competitive pressures. The regulatory agencies, in effect, try to prevent the monopolies from behaving like monopolies. We shall shortly see why this is important.

To summarize briefly: the advantages of mass production, or economies of scale, engender oligopoly and, in extreme form, monopoly; the advantages of mass marketing reinforce, and in many cases replace, the effects of economies of scale.

Mass Marketing

Mass marketing is a phenomenon quite alien to competition, and of very recent origin. The discovery is generally attributed to the National Biscuit Company, which launched a product called "Uneeda Biscuits" about 70 years ago and thereby consigned to a nostalgic past the old cracker barrel filled with crackers from small, anonymous bakeries. No recent discovery, save only the automobile, has had so deep and pervasive an impact on our way of life.

Mass marketing consists in distinguishing a firm's products from those of its competitors by means of branding and trademarks, and in creating a preference for the brand by advertising. The interplay among mass marketing, mass production, and the formation of oligopoly is very intricate. Mass marketing depends on the identification of a product with its producer.[3] In an oligopoly based on decreasing long-run costs, this identification arises spontaneously: when only a half-dozen firms manufacture a product, purchasers come to know which one made each article; the manufacturer's signature is on every item he produces, be it in the form of merely his firm name or in the form of an elaborately concocted trademark. In these circumstances the firm might as well turn the inevitable to advantage, and try to make consumers *want* his particular brand of the commodity.

[2] A *trust* is a corporate device in which the stockholders of a number of oligopolistic firms assign their shares to an organization that holds them "in trust" and is thus able to control the firms and coordinate their policies. See pp. 56-57 of Richard Caves, *American Industry: Structure, Conduct, Performance,* 2nd ed., in this Series.

[3] The contrasting anonymity of producers in a competitive industry is illustrated by women's dresses. If a woman likes the looks and price of a dress, she buys it, and she rarely knows or cares which company manufactured it except in the case of *haute couture.*

This opportunity is also almost a necessity because of the economics of large-scale production and the nature of the rivalry among competing oligopolists. Mass production requires an elaborate plant with heavy fixed costs, and so a large volume of sales is imperative. The owner of a large plant cannot afford to entrust his sales volume to the caprices of an anonymous market where even a high-cost, pip-squeak competitor can steal sales from him, or a respectable rival can attract his customers with ease. He must tie his customers to himself as firmly as he can. And this is where mass merchandizing helps, because it is one of the most effective expedients available to oligopolists in their struggle to attract each other's customers and hold their own. So oligopoly, which makes mass merchandizing possible, also makes it necessary.

But mass merchandizing can succeed even when there is no technological basis for oligopoly; it can create oligopoly singlehandedly. This comes about through a number of mechanisms, of which the most evident is the existence of economies of scale in advertising. If a firm doubles the number of insertions of an advertisement or advertises in media with double the circulation of media previously used, certainly its advertising costs will approximately double, but the effectiveness of its campaign will more than double. The psychological causes of this phenomenon are obscure, but it seems that repeated exposures to a firm's advertisements reinforce each other. Advertising men say "Repetition is reputation." It appears that an advertising campaign leaves a residue of feeling of familiarity that makes the customer assured and comfortable when he buys the product, and uncertain and dubious when he confronts an unadvertised article. And customers sometimes believe that if a firm spends a great deal on advertising, it cannot afford to offer an inferior product. But be these as they may, single or rare exposure to a firm's advertisments do not predispose the consumer to purchase; frequent exposures in large-circulation media do. This gives large advertising campaigns, and the large firms that can afford them, marked advantages. It conduces to oligopoly.

Moreover, success in selling is self-reinforcing. When prospective purchasers see people all around them using a particular brand, they presume that it gives satisfactory, and perhaps even superior, service. This is the *demonstration effect*. Because of it each sale makes the next one a bit easier. It is a boon to the large firms whose products are visible everywhere, helping them grow while the smaller, less well-known firms find it difficult to attract the consumer's attention to their brands. Any disparity in the size of firms tends to increase rather than to shrink.

Finally, large volume is the key that unlocks the channels of distribution. Some products, such as automobiles and gasoline, are marketed through franchised dealers and chains of brand outlets (respectively). For such products the volume of sales in each locality served must be large enough to support an outlet of minimum efficient scale. The number of outlets must in turn be great enough to provide convenient service to customers throughout the region in which the product is sold—frequently the entire country (to gain the advantages of national advertising). Multiplying the required level of sales per outlet by a large number of outlets leads to a requirement for selling to a substantial proportion of the entire market, and again, this is the essence of oligopoly.

Large volume is also essential to products distributed through general re-

95

tailers. The consumer is most likely to buy what he sees; namely, what is on the dealers' shelves. Dealers, in turn, assign their scarce shelf-space to brands that are selling well. Thus, large volume helps generate still larger volume. Here is yet another self-reinforcing mechanism, and all these mechanisms reinforce each other. In short, bigness *per se* is an advantage to a firm: large firms grow and small ones vanish or are relegated to narrow, specialized segments of the market.[4]

To recap: in many industries the advantages of mass production and mass merchandising conspire to concentrate the market in a few large hands. Since the ultimate in concentration—monopoly—is impeded by legal restraint, it is not surprising that oligopoly has become the characteristic form of market in modern, industrial economies; practically all the famous companies you can name are oligopolists. We must now investigate the performance of these two market forms. Monopoly, being simpler, comes first.

MONOPOLY

Everyone envies the happy monopolist. The competitive firm has to sell at the market price, and squeeze out what profits it can by holding production costs down to their very minimum—but even then is likely to have its profits competed away. The oligopolist has formidable rivals to contend with. But the monopolist chooses his own prices and has no serious rivals; indeed, he has practically nothing to worry about except the Anti-Trust Division, or perhaps a regulatory commission. How should he conduct himself to take advantage of this unparalleled felicity?

The answer is basically a familiar one by now, but we have to introduce a new concept to express it clearly. The essential peculiarity of the monopolist is that his firm's individual demand curve is identical with the demand curve for his product. The monopolist has the privilege of setting the price of his product, but then he can sell only the quantity corresponding to that price on his product's demand curve. If he raises the price he must be content to sell less; if he wants to sell more he must lower the price. So his essential decision problem is to find the most profitable price-quantity pair on his demand curve. He does this by the now-familiar process of equating his margins—by equating the marginal cost of his product to the increase in his gross sales revenue that would result from selling one more unit. This is the concept we need, the concept of *marginal revenue*.[5]

Marginal revenue is the increase in the gross value of sales that would result from selling one more unit.

The distinctive feature of a monopoly is that a monopolist's marginal revenue is *not* equal to his price, as is a competitive firm's. For the monopolist to sell an additional unit he must reduce the price on all units sold, in accordance with the slope of his demand curve.[6] Hence the amount he realizes by selling an additional

[4] Magazine publishing is a prime example of these reinforcing mechanisms. The result is a handful of general-circulation giants such as Time-Life, Inc., and the Curtis Publishing Company, along with thousands of smaller—though often quite respectable—firms catering to specialized and localized markets. (These smaller firms are called "the competitive fringe.")

[5] The exact symmetry between marginal revenue and marginal cost should be noted.

[6] There is such a thing as a "discriminating monopolist," one who is in a position to charge different prices for different units of output. This is even better than monopoly *simpliciter*. The average renowned surgeon is in this happy position, for example, and so are most electric utility companies and railroads. But we shall not be able to study the behavior of discriminating monopolists.

unit is less than the price he sells it for; reduction in the price of his previous sales has to be subtracted off. For a monopolist, though not for a competitor, then, we must distinguish between price and marginal revenue.

It should be pretty evident why it is most profitable for a monopolist to select the volume of sales at which marginal revenue equals marginal cost. If marginal revenue is greater than marginal cost, selling one more unit will contribute more to his sales revenues than producing it will add to his expenses. It will enhance his profits. On the other hand, if marginal revenue is less than marginal cost, he is losing money on the last unit he produces, and perhaps on others. But when marginal revenue is equal to marginal cost, he cannot increase his profits either by reducing or increasing his levels of output and sales.

From a competitive firm's point of view, the demand curve for his product is too remote to be of interest; no conceivable increase in his level of sales could have a visible effect on the total sales of the industry or on the market price. But a monopolist realizes that he can depress the price by his own activities, and this makes increases in output less attractive to him than to a competitive firm.

To see the force of all this, suppose that a monopolist can sell 800 units a month at a price of $13 per unit and that his demand curve shows that he has to reduce his price by $\frac{5}{8} \not c$ in order to sell 801 units a month. Then, with an output of 800 units a month, his total value of sales is $800 \times \$13 = \$10,400$; with an output of 801 units a month his total value of sales is $801 \times (\$13 - \$.00625) = \$10,407.99$. Note that his *marginal revenue* is about $8, which is substantially less than the price of $13 which he is charging.

Whether the monopolist will want to increase his monthly sales from 800 to 801 depends on the comparison of this marginal revenue with his marginal cost. If his marginal cost at an output of 800 a month is *less* than $8 per unit, it will be profitable for him to increase his production. But if his marginal cost is *more* than $8 a unit, even though it is less than his price of $13 a unit, he will want to reduce his output to 799 a month (which would permit him to raise his price about $\frac{5}{8} \not c$ per unit), or even further. He will be content with sales of 800 a month only if his marginal cost is just about $8 a unit. In general:

> A monopolist will choose a price-quantity combination on his demand curve at which his marginal revenue is equal to his marginal cost.

This is the salient difference between competition and monopoly: the competitor and the monopolist both produce outputs such that marginal revenue equals marginal cost, but a competitor's marginal revenue is equal to his price, while a monopolist's is inevitably less. We shall soon see the consequence of this.

A Graphic Representation of Monopoly

The behavior of a monopolist can be analyzed with the help of a convenient diagram. To help construct it, imagine a monopolist whose cost data are the same as those of the competitive firm discussed in Chapter 3 and shown in Table 3-1. (For convenience, those cost data are reproduced in Table 6-1 and graphed in Figure 6-1.) A monopolist does not confront a market price, but he does have to consider the demand curve for his product, for this shows how many units he can sell at each price that he might select. This curve also is shown in Fig. 6-1.[7]

Table 6-1 COST AND REVENUE DATA FOR A MONOPOLIST

Monthly Output (Units)	Average Cost ($)	($/Unit) Marginal Cost ($)	Price ($)	Marginal Revenue ($)
100	19.00	—	17.375	16.74375
200	13.00	7.00	16.750	15.49375
300	10.67	6.00	16.125	14.24375
400	9.50	6.00	15.500	12.99375
500	8.80	6.00	14.875	11.74375
600	8.42	6.50	14.250	10.49375
700	8.21	7.00	13.625	9.24375
800	8.19	8.00	13.000	7.99375
900	8.33	9.50	12.375	6.74375
1000	8.65	11.50	11.750	5.49375
1100	9.14	14.00	11.125	4.24375

The worthwhileness of an additional sale per month to a monopolist does not depend upon its price but upon the marginal revenue that it yields, and we already know that this will be less than the price. The marginal revenue corresponding to each level of sales is also shown in the figure.[8]

The marginal-revenue and marginal-cost curves intersect at an output of 800 units a month. (The average-cost curve is irrelevant for the moment.) By our previous reasoning, this is the most profitable output for the monopolist, so that he should charge the corresponding price on the demand curve, or $13. If he should charge a higher price (sell fewer units) he would be declining to produce some units that would add more to his revenue than to his costs, because for them, marginal revenue would exceed marginal cost. If he should charge a lower price,

[7] The formula for the demand curve in the graph is $p = 18 - (x/160)$. That formula shows the price, p, at which consumers will purchase any given monthly volume, x. Try $x = 1,200$. You should get $p = \$10.50$ for the price at which 1,200 units a month will be bought.

[8] The marginal revenue resulting from an additional sale at any level is a consequence of the demand curve in the following way. At any level of sales the total revenue, call it $TR(x)$, equals quantity time price, or $xp(x)$, where we write $p(x)$ for p to remind ourselves that p depends on x. Thus:

$$TR(x) = xp(x) = x\left(18 - \frac{x}{160}\right)$$

Then, by the definition of marginal revenue:

$$MR(x) = TR(x+1) - TR(x)$$

$$= (x+1)\, 18 - \left(\frac{x+1}{160}\right)$$

$$- x\left(18 - \frac{x}{160}\right)$$

$$= 18 - \frac{x+1}{160} - x\frac{x+1}{160} + x\frac{x}{160}$$

$$= 18 - \frac{2x+1}{160}$$

(Compute the marginal revenue for $x = 800$. It should be $7.99375.) $MR(x)$ is the marginal-revenue curve shown in the diagram.

he would be selling some units that cost him more than their contribution to his sales revenue. Only $13 is just right.

How about his profit at this most profitable level of output? Profit arises from the excess of price over average cost. It so happens, in this instance, that the average and marginal costs are equal at the most profitable level of output. (We shall see shortly why the data were chosen to work out that way.) Therefore, marginal revenue is equal to average cost, and since price is necessarily greater than marginal revenue, there is a positive profit—the monopolist's profit.

But, we should emphasize, the data didn't *have* to work out that way. The most profitable level of output, determined by the intersection of the marginal-cost and revenue curves, might have occurred in the rising portion of the average-cost curve. In that case, marginal cost would have been greater than average cost, and price, being greater than marginal revenue (= marginal cost), would have been greater still. Finally, the most profitable level of output might have occurred in the

FIG. 6-1 Short-run equilibrium of a monopolist. The price is higher than it would be for a competitor, and the quantity is smaller.

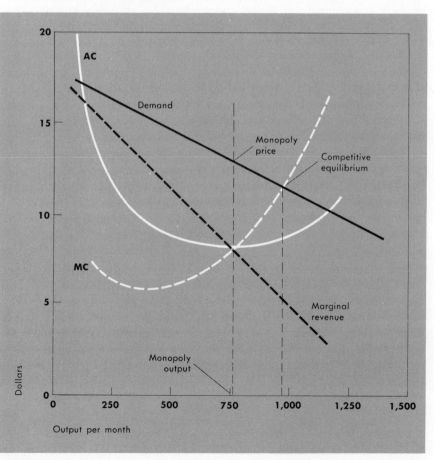

falling portion of the average-cost curve. Then marginal cost and marginal revenue would be less than average cost. But the price, which exceeds the marginal revenue, could still be greater than the average cost, leaving a positive profit.

Monopoly in the Long Run

In the short run, then, the monopolist with a given fixed plant operates at the level of output at which marginal revenue and marginal cost are equal. His long-run adjustments are then very much like those of a competitive firm. Having attained the most profitable level of output in the short run, the monopolist will enlarge, reduce, or modify his plant if by doing so he can reduce the average cost of his current level of output. In the long run, therefore, he will have the plant in which his current output can be produced as cheaply as possible.

If the monopolist's technology is one with constant long-run costs, then, just as in a competitive industry, when he has the most appropriate plant for his current output, he will also be using that plant at its most efficient level: the bottom of its average-cost curve. This is the situation depicted in Fig. 6-1, which accordingly shows the long-run equilibrium of a monopolist with constant long-run costs. By contrast with the competitive case, in which profit is competed away in the long run, a substantial margin of profit remains for the monopolist.

We know, however, that monopoly typically tends to arise in a different sort of industry, one characterized by decreasing long-run costs. The situation shown in Fig. 6-2 is therefore much more characteristic of monopolies. In that figure, the curve labeled *AC* is a long-run, average-cost curve—that is, a curve showing the

FIG. 6-2 Long-run equilibrium of a monopolist with decreasing long-run costs. Price is inevitably higher than marginal cost.

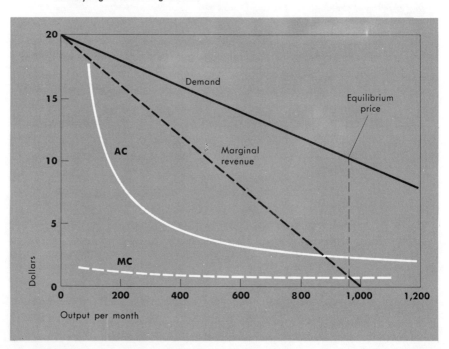

average cost for each level of output when produced in the plant in which that cost is lowest. (Note that it declines throughout its range.) The corresponding marginal-cost curve is also shown; it is always below the average cost curve. (Why?) This diagram makes it clear that a monopolist cannot be blamed for behaving like a monopolist. Since his marginal cost is always lower than his average cost, if he were to charge a price equal to marginal cost, as a competitor does, he would be losing money. No matter how economists may extoll the virtues of marginal cost pricing (i.e., charging for each unit of a product the addition to costs attributable to it), the monopolist cannot afford to follow that policy.

Demand and marginal-revenue curves are also shown in Fig. 6-2. The long-run equilibrium for this monopolist is to produce about 960 units a month for a marginal cost of 68¢ and a price of $10.40. A regulatory agency might require the monopolist to charge a price equal to average cost, interpreting cost to include a reasonable return on invested capital; and this is often done. In this instance, however, extrapolating the data in Fig. 6-2 shows that such a regulation would result in an output of 1,850 units, a price of $1.50, and a marginal cost of 54¢. Although the monopolistic restriction of output would be greatly reduced, the principle of marginal-cost pricing would still be violated.

Monopoly and Elasticity of Demand

What makes monopoly possible is the efficiency of large-scale operation; what makes it worthwhile is the slope of the demand curve. For remember: the more nearly horizontal a monopolist's demand curve is, the closer together are his demand and marginal-revenue curves, and the smaller is the discrepancy between price and marginal cost. If a monopolist could have an absolutely horizontal demand curve, he would behave just like a competitor. The difference between competitive and monopolistic behavior therefore depends on the slope of the demand curve. Perhaps we had better see in a bit more detail how this slope influences the monopolist.

For this purpose, the most significant characteristic of a demand curve is its *elasticity,* a very natural measure of how responsive demand is to changes in price.

> The elasticity of demand for a commodity is the percentage reduction in the volume of sales that would be induced by a 1 per cent increase in price.

To illustrate this concept, let us compute the elasticity of demand for the monopolized product of Table 6-1 when 800 units are being sold. The price is then $13, and a 1 per cent increase would raise it to $13.13. From the formula for the demand curve (footnote 7, above) we can compute that 779 units would be sold if this price were charged. This is a fall of 21 units or 2.6 per cent, which accordingly is the elasticity.

The critical value of elasticity is unity, or one. For if elasticity $= 1$, then a 1 per cent increase in price will cause a 1 per cent decrease in the volume of sales. These two changes will just about offset each other, leaving the total value of sales unchanged. But with 1 per cent fewer units to be produced, total variable costs would be diminished by such a change. It follows that if a monopolist should find himself producing an output for which the elasticity of demand is unity or lower, he would restrict his output and increase his price. As he does so, his elasticity of demand will increase, generally speaking (but not inevitably). This is illustrated in Table 6-2, which is derived from Table 6-1 by the computation just explained. The monopolist will stop raising his price, as we already know, when he has restricted output to the point where marginal revenue and marginal cost are equal.

Table 6-2 ELASTICITY OF DEMAND DERIVED FROM A LINEAR DEMAND CURVE

Monthly Output (Units)	Price ($)	Marginal Revenue ($)	Elasticity
100	17.38	16.744	27.8
200	16.75	15.494	13.4
300	16.12	14.244	8.6
400	15.50	12.994	6.2
500	14.88	11.744	4.8
600	14.25	10.494	3.8
700	13.62	9.244	3.1
800	13.00	7.994	2.6
900	12.38	6.744	2.2
1000	11.75	5.494	1.9
1100	11.12	4.244	1.6
—	—	—	—
1440	9.00	−0.006	1.0

It is shown in the appendix to this chapter that when this equality is attained, the percentage markup of price over marginal cost, from which the monopolist's profit is derived, is equal to the reciprocal of the elasticity of demand. If the elasticity of demand is high, this percentage markup is small; if demand is inelastic it is large. The profitability of a monopoly depends, therefore, directly on the elasticity of the demand curve.

The Consequences of Monopoly

In effect, the monopolist restricts his output to maintain his price. Some monopolists, recognizing this, do not even bother to set a price openly. De Beers Consolidated, Ltd., the world monopolist of gem-quality diamonds, simply controls the output of its subsidiaries and allows the price to be determined by a kind of auction of this controlled output. They get the desired result without the bother and embarrassment of having to publish an elaborate price schedule.

If by some miracle the industry graphed in Fig. 6-1 could be converted to a competitive industry with the same cost and demand conditions, the principles of Chapter 3 would apply. Each competitor would ignore, correctly, the effect on the price of an expansion of his sales, and output would rise until the marginal cost was as great as the price. If this industry were competitive, therefore, output would increase to 1,000 units a month and the price would fall to $11.60.

The fundamental objection to monopoly is that by holding down production to the level at which marginal cost equals his marginal revenue, the monopolist wastes economic resources. It is important to see why this is so. When the output is 800 units a month, the marginal cost is $8 per unit. This means that an 801st unit could be produced by purchasing and using labor services, raw materials, power, and other ingredients worth, in all, $8. The fact that the monopolist would have to pay $8 for these ingredients indicates that other firms—especially including competitive ones—are willing to pay that much for them; otherwise the price would be different. This indeed is the true meaning of prices: what one man *has to* pay for something is what another one *would be* willing to pay for it.

Now, why would a competitive firm be willing to pay $8 for these resources? Because it could use them to produce something worth $8 to its customers, thereby adding $8 to its total sales. (Remember that in a competitive industry price equals marginal cost, so that a product that adds $x to costs will sell for $x.) We have encountered again the notion of opportunity costs—the idea that the real cost of anything is the value of the things that could have been produced with the resources it consumes. The opportunity cost of the monopolist's unproduced 801st unit, for which customers are willing to pay about $12.99, is only $8, and herein lies the waste. Since the customers would be willing to pay $12.99 for the unavailable 801st unit, they clearly prefer it to the $8 worth of alternatives that are produced in its stead. By declining to produce the 801st unit, the monopolist has compelled the economy to use certain resources to produce something worth only $8 when he could have used those resources to produce something worth $12.99. The monopolist has barred some resources from their most productive employment.

We can look at this same distortion in another way: by pegging the price at $13, the monopolist has put a false signal into the price system. From the standpoint of his customers, the opportunity cost of his product is $13 because that is the value of the other things they have to forego in order to obtain a unit of it; from the standpoint of the economy the opportunity cost is $8. Consumers therefore unduly restrict their use of the monopolized product. Perhaps they use an inferior substitute for it that costs $11 to produce, thereby consuming $11 worth of resources for a purpose that could be served better by $8 worth. Consumers are misled, from the point of view of making the best use of the resources available to the economy, into buying too little of the monopolized product, and too much of others.

For the foregoing reasons, among others, unregulated monopoly is generally considered to be intolerable. But in the public service industries,[9] especially, the economies of scale are so striking that it seems almost inconceivable to have several firms serving a single area or route. Consequently, in these industries it is usual to permit a monopoly subject to government supervision. Unfortunately, we cannot discuss in detail here the problems of regulating a public service monopoly; it would be instructive to do so.[10] Suffice it to say that they all arise from the extraordinary difficulty of making sound economic decisions without the guidance of market prices. (A regulatory commission has, in effect, to set the price schedule of the industry it supervises. This alone is hard enough, since, as we have seen, marginal costs are not an adequate guide. But on top of that, once this has been

---

[9] Telephone and telegraph, electric power, gas, railroad and air transport, pipelines, urban transit, and the like.
[10] Some of the difficulties are considered in pp. 68-73 of Richard Caves, *American Industry: Structure, Conduct, Performance,* 2nd ed., in this Series.

accomplished, the commission usually finds that the quality of service that it expected will not be provided at the set prices without incessant supervision, because of the absence of competitive pressures.)

OLIGOPOLY

Oligopoly is not a compromise between competition and monopoly; it is fundamentally different. Competition and monopoly have this in common: that each firm confronts impersonal and anonymous market forces. A competitive firm knows that nothing it does will have a noticeable effect on the profitability or behavior of any other firm, and that no other firm can affect its profits significantly. A monopolist deals with numerous customers, no one of whom has an appreciable influence on his sales or profits. But an oligopolist stands in a different relationship both with his competitors and with his customers.

With respect to the oligopolist's competitors: there are only a few of them, and so whenever he changes his price, alters his product, or does anything else of that sort, the move is noticed and the impact is felt by the other firms in the market. Because they may be induced to retaliate in some manner, the oligopolist must weigh carefully the pros and cons of his moves. The inescapable fact is that the profits of an oligopolist depend not only on what he does, but on what each of his rivals does, and vice-versa. We shall shortly explore the consequences of this interdependency.

With respect to his customers: the oligopolist, being one of but a few suppliers, lacks the anonymity of the true competitor. (We have already noted some of the far-reaching implications that follow from this.) Indeed, the identification of the oligopolist with his product is so important that it pays to distinguish two variants of this market structure: *differentiated* and *undifferentiated* oligopoly.

In a differentiated oligopoly the products of different firms are distinguished clearly and purchasers have definite preferences among them. In undifferentiated oligopoly, purchasers have no strong preferences among producers.

The oligopolist prefers differentiated to undifferentiated oligopoly. To the extent that he succeeds in differentiating his product, his customers regard competing brands as inferior substitutes, and he attains the position of a weak monopolist with some inelasticity in his demand curve to exploit. Well differentiated brands (e.g., Cadillacs, Parker pens) can sell for more money than can comparable competing products. So the oligopolist strives to differentiate, and for this purpose has two devices: advertising (which we have already discussed) and *product variation* (by which the oligopolist endeavors to incorporate "selling features" into his product, in order to make it better, or at least different).

The development of selling features that appeal to customers is one of the main bases for the claim of the merchandising profession that it makes a positive social contribution—a claim that is difficult to appraise. Some very sardonic remarks used to be made about high tail-fins on automobiles (though they did make it possible for a driver to see the rear of his own car for once), but the same critics had almost nothing derogatory to say about the introduction of automatic shifting (which gave mechanics nightmares and reduced gasoline efficiency by more than 10 per cent). Fundamentally, it would seem that the critics had no

104

basis for judging that one of these changes was "progress," the other not; consumers accepted both gladly.[11] What we are driving at, is that these and all such changes are very costly: it has been estimated that the frequent model changes in the automobile industry cost about $1 billion a year.[12] Are the improvements worth it? You have to judge yourself.

Products differ in the extent to which they can be differentiated. It happens to be extraordinarily difficult to devise really substantial technical improvements that competing brands cannot easily imitate (though there are occasional exceptions). Therefore, product differences exist mostly in the mind of the customer, and it is much easier to insinuate them into the minds of untrained consumers than into the minds of hard-bitten purchasing agents, who tend to concentrate on price and serviceability. The essential contrast can be visualized by comparing the tactics to be used in selling an automobile fleet to the purchasing agent of a large firm, with those most effective in selling a single car to his wife. The result is that differentiated oligopoly is most characteristic of products sold to ultimate consumers, while undifferentiated oligopoly is common in industrial products.

From all this it should be clear that an oligopolist's concerns and methods are very different from those of an anonymous competitor. An oligopolist's primary concern is with his sales strategy. His firm stands or falls with his success in attracting sales without changing price, a situation which is quite alien to all other market forms. His situation is complicated by the fact that his competitors will not stand idly by while he does his best: they will ape his innovations, make some of their own, and match his advertising campaigns with theirs. We must now turn back to the strategic interrelationships among oligopolists.

Oligopolistic Strategy

To recap: whether his product is differentiated or not, an oligopolist has a handful of competitors to worry about. What each of them does affects him, as what he does affects each of them. This mutual interdependence sets up a very complicated relationship.

Such a situation, in which there are several participants with conflicting interests, each of whom has significant influence on the attainments of the others as well as on his own outcome, is known as a *game of strategy*—or, for short, as a *game*. (Chess and other board exercises are one sort of game; oligopoly—like international diplomacy, labor-management negotiations, and so on—is a game of quite another sort, but subject to analysis by remarkably similar methods.) The crucial feature of any game is that each participant bases his decisions on what he expects the others to do, and therefore on what he thinks the others expect him to do, and indeed on what he thinks the others think he expects them to do, and so on. Can anything useful be said about such complicated situations? Well, sometimes.

Consider this case—about the simplest game conceivable. Firms *A* and *B* make virtually identical products. Each spends $1 million a year to keep its

---

[11] It so happened, of course, that one of these changes became permanent and the other proved evanescent. Perhaps this provides a basis for belated appraisal.

[12] See also p. 111 in Richard Caves, *American Industry: Structure, Conduct, Performance,* 2nd ed., in this Series.

customers from deserting to the other. Actually, they could reduce their advertising budgets to $200,000 without hurting their sales, and each would be $800,000 better off. But if *A* cut his advertising budget unilaterally, he would lose sales to *B* on which he made a profit of $1,200,000 a year. The result of this unilateral action would be, then, to reduce *A's* profit by $400,000 and to increase *B's* by $1,200,000. Firm *B* is exactly symmetrically situated. These data are summarized in Table 6-3,

Table 6-3 PAYOFF MATRIX FOR ADVERTISING GAME
(Entries show A's gain/B's gain in $1,000, compared with status quo)

Firm B's Advertising Budget	Firm A's Advertising Budget	
	$1,000,000	$200,000
$1,000,000	0/0	−400/1200
$ 200,000	1200/−400	800/800

called the *payoff matrix* of this game. For example, it is shown there that if *A* cuts his advertising expenditures to $200,000 while *B* continues at the current level, then *A's* profits will be $400,000 less than at present while *B's* will be $1,200,000 greater.

A's decision is very, very easy, and *B's* is the same. For there are only two possibilities permitted, and both point in the same direction. If *B* maintains his current budget, then *A* will lose $400,000 by cutting his. If *B* cuts his budget, then *A* is $400,000 better off if he retains his than if he cuts. In short, *A* should retain the high level of expenditure, whatever *B* does, and *B* should behave the same, and this in spite of the fact that both would be better off if they could mutually agree to cut back. (The analogy with armaments races is striking.)[13]

The game we just played was especially simple because although the two firms' profits were interconnected, their decisions were not; the best decision for each remained the same irrespective of what the other did. But another simple example will illustrate that this needn't always be the case. Again there is a pair of oligopolists who are required by industry custom to announce simultaneously their prices for the next season. They cannot communicate with each other beforehand, either because of mutual antipathy or for fear of the Antitrust Division. Demand is strong and inelastic, so that if both announce price increases, both will enjoy profit increases of $100,000 for the season. If, however, only one increases his price, he will lose sales to the other and his profits will decline by $50,000 while the firm that stands pat will gain $50,000. The situation is summarized in Table 6-4.

Clearly, both firms are best off if both increase prices. But suppose you were firm *A:* would you do it? Remember that you would thereby run the risk of losing $50,000 if your opponent stood pat. There are two circumstances under which you would not increase your price: (1) if you were a conservative manager for

---

[13] Let us emphasize again that this is the very simplest, and therefore the least interesting, game situation known. For a lively introduction to more interesting games see J. D. Williams, *The Compleat Strategyst* (New York: McGraw-Hill Book Co., 1954).

Even this simple game, known as "the prisoners' dilemma," has its paradoxical side, as we saw, and has a surprising variety of applications to economics and sociology. It is analyzed further in R. D. Luce and H. Raiffa, *Games and Decisions* (New York: John Wiley & Co., 1957), pp. 94-99.

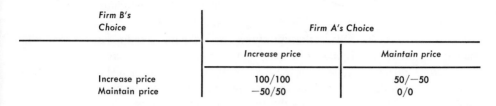

Table 6-4 **PAYOFF MATRIX FOR PRICE-CHANGE GAME**
(Entries shown A's gain/B's gain in $1,000, compared with status quo)

Firm B's Choice	Firm A's Choice	
	Increase price	*Maintain price*
Increase price	100/100	50/—50
Maintain price	—50/50	0/0

whom the hope of gaining $100,000 wasn't worth the risk and worry of possibly losing $50,000; and (2) if you believed that firm *B* was under conservative management and would not assume the risks of a price increase. Indeed, there is a third circumstance that leads to the same decision, and that suggests how subtly one has to reason when money is at stake. It is (3) if you believed that firm *B* believed that you were a conservative firm and would therefore not raise your price.[14] So it is far from certain that the firms would make mutually advantageous decisions if they were not allowed to communicate.

These two trivial games suggest one ingredient of life in an oligopoly: the strategic interplay among the rivals. In practice, the games oligopolists play are far more complicated. Each firm may have to contend with the actions of several confreres rather than only one, and each will have a range of alternatives with respect to prices, product design, merchandising policy, and many other things, instead of only a single dichotomy. On top of that, the inevitable uncertainties of business make it impossible to write down a sure-fire matrix, as we have done.

But the crucial complication that we have neglected is that every decision an oligopolist makes has two effects. One is the direct, intended consequence that is recorded in the payoff matrix. The other is the information or impression that is conveyed to the other oligopolists in the market. The price-change example shows how important this second aspect is; it is important therein for each firm to impress upon its rival that it is willing to take a chance. Communication is relevant in the advertising example, too, though less obviously. Thus, firm *A* in that example might well cut its advertising budget and sustain its $400,000 loss in the hope of communicating to firm *B* that it is prepared to cooperate if that firm cuts its budget.[15]

The communications aspect of oligopolistic strategy is used in many ways. An important one is that a prominent firm will teach its rivals not to cut price by responding promptly to every price cut by a slightly deeper one. It also complicates

---

[14] Notice that this opinion on firm *B's* part is likely to be self-confirming, even if erroneous. You can follow out these lines of reasoning much further if you want to. But things can be even more confusing if there is no mutually advantageous pair of decisions— and there need not be any.

[15] We don't know of any instance where this has actually happened in the field of advertising. A few years ago, though, there was an instructive episode in the automobile industry. The manufacturers managed to cut back on horsepower ratings by such *tacit bargaining*. The improvement—and it was an improvement from everybody's point of view, teen-agers excepted —did not last because the "agreement" was unenforceable. The manufacturers in relatively weak market positions broke the industry discipline in the hope of making some inroads, and the market leaders were forced to follow.

oligopolistic behavior by making every move ambiguous.[16] If one oligopolist reduces his price, the others must conjecture whether he is trying to tell them that the time is ripe for reducing the industry's price structure, or whether he is aggressively trying to increase his market share. Even the best-intentioned price cut, if misinterpreted, may touch off a price war, and an oligopolist thinks at least twice before running this risk. Oligopolists often try to avoid this risk by making surreptitious price cuts, either quietly granting discounts from list prices, or not charging for quality improvements. But such subterfuges do little more than delay retaliation, since customers have proved to be very poor at keeping them secret.

Two implications follow. In the first place, the convenient distinction between short-run and long-run decisions is obscured in oligopoly since every move, by changing the rivals' assessment of the firm's intentions and situation, has long-run consequences. In the second place, since the risks and uncertainties of every move are greatly enhanced, oligopolists become reluctant to initiate *any* changes. Oligopoly is a peculiarly sticky and rigid form of market.

Oligopolies in Practice

We have seen that oligopoly is almost inevitable in industries that rely on modern technology, but that it is an unresponsive form of market in which firms cannot react readily to changes in market conditions, or even pursue their mutual advantage. Obviously it is far from an ideal state of affairs—but then, social institutions do have ways of adapting themselves to such challenges, and oligopoly is no exception.

The ideal way out, for the oligopolists, is to cooperate with each other. In the late nineteenth century, when oligopoly first became important, it showed strong tendencies to break down into monopoly. The original oligopolists in steel, tobacco, oil refining, tin-can manufacture, and many other industries merged into trusts and cartels to reap the advantages (to them) of monopoly. The antitrust movement on the part of the government, however, soon either impeded this trend or forced it underground. Oligopolists then turned to semiformal consultations, such as the "Judge Gary Dinners" in the steel industry,[17] but these too were disallowed by the courts.

Beaten by the bench, and anxious to avoid further scrutiny and unfavorable publicity, oligopolists were forced to rely on more circumspect methods of cooperation. These depended heavily on the tacit bargaining mentioned above, and on the observance and enforcement of unwritten behavioral conventions. The most ubiquitous of these conventions was that price competition was disallowed— and to this day oligopolists contest bitterly with each other by advertising, by product variation, by expense-account entertainment, by industrial espionage, and by every other expedient that ingenuity can invent, but they do not cut prices.[18] Price-cutting is a weapon that is too readily available, and too destructive to all concerned.

16 Just like bidding in bridge. In bridge, elaborate conventions have been introduced to clarify the meaning of bids. We shall see that something very similar occurs in oligopoly.

17 See Walter Adams (ed.), *The Structure of American Industry* (New York: Macmillan, 1961), Chapter 5.

18 A famous example of this behavioral convention in practice occurred in 1956, when Chevrolet and Ford were vigorously contending for market leadership. When the prices for the 1957 model year were announced, Ford discovered that its prices were 3 per cent below those of Chevrolet. Ford promptly raised its prices. Evidently both firms realized that price competition could do nothing but harm to both, rivalry or no rivalry.

This makes the price changes that are inevitable from time to time a very delicate matter. By far the most common way to handle the matter is through the convention of price leadership: one prominent firm, often but not always the largest in the industry, is accepted as the one with the responsibility for initiating price changes for all to follow. Now, although this prevents misunderstandings, the price leader remains, as it were, a king who rules on sufferance. He may lead, but if the move is not generally advantageous, perhaps no one will follow. And sometimes his price leadership is contested—particularly when a price reduction seems more urgent to his followers than it does to him. The continued maintenance of the leader's reign depends heavily on general acquiescence in the current distribution of market shares; when some of the firms vie vigorously to improve their positions in the market, or struggle desperately to survive, the peace is likely to be fragile. In short, an oligopoly with an established price-leader is not the same as a monopoly—the leader's freedom of action is much more circumscribed.

No one really knows how oligopolists decide on a new schedule of prices when the need for a change has been recognized. There has been much testimony on this subject, before congressional committees and on other occasions, and what the oligopolists say is always much the same: they compute their prices by estimating long-run average costs and adding a markup that will allow them a reasonable profit on their invested capital. This "rule" is too vague to mean much. It does not say what volume of sales is to be used in estimating average costs, nor how one decides on a "reasonable profit," nor how the price structure is to be preserved when the price that is appropriate for one firm is either excessive or insufficient for others. In fact, the rule is perverse; it implies that prices should be raised when sales are slack, to cover fixed costs. Close questioning, not surprisingly, discloses that the "rule" has to be interpreted "in the light of competitive conditions," and that there are numerous exceptions to it. What this all probably means is that the formula gives a first approximation to prices, which are then adjusted in conformity to strategic considerations that are too varied and subtle to be explained to congressmen and the lay public.

A plausible hypothesis, though one very hard to confirm, is that the price leaders act like monopolists on behalf of the entire industry. That is, they recognize the industry demand curve and the cost curves of the average firm, and attempt to set a price that will afford such a firm the largest possible profits. In following this policy the price setter is not being altruistic to his competitors; his task is to propose a price schedule that will be followed. He must take into account the fact that one that favors himself unduly is likely to lead to disruptive retaliation, especially if he is either a low-cost firm (such as General Motors) or a high-cost one (such as U. S. Steel). Even the interests of the competitive fringe must be considered for they, too, can upset the delicate balance of power.

In this clumsy way an oligopolistic industry retains a rough contact with the conditions of production and the desires of its customers. When production costs and prices threaten to become excessively out of line, a readjustment takes place only belatedly and reluctantly—hopefully before temptations and unrelieved pressures induce the individual firms to break oligopolistic discipline and "demoralize **109** the market."

The upshot is that oligopoly is an awkward market form. It is unresponsive to day-to-day and week-to-week changes in market conditions. Since the oligopolist is too inflexible to adjust to minor market fluctuations, he has to ride out the ups and downs in the hope of averaging out correctly over the long pull. But this hope is doomed to disappointment. If the industry cannot respond via price changes to the current state of market conditions, neither can its customers; consumers are not reliably induced either to use oligopolists' products when they are plentiful, or to refrain from using them when they are scarce. The oligopolists themselves experience inefficient fluctuations in their volumes of production and sales, and some of the productive resources of the economy are wasted.

AN APPRAISAL OF MARKETS

In this chapter we have considered two common alternatives to competition: monopoly and oligopoly. Monopoly, we noticed, causes economic waste (and perhaps some injustice, the ill effects of which fortunately can be moderated by regulation). Oligopolists, caught between economic necessities and legal restrictions, are not able to perform efficiently from either their point of view or the economy's. Nevertheless these market forms are needed to take advantage of modern technology.

The purpose of all markets is to transmit information. The firms themselves are organized to do the substantive work of the economy: to produce, store, transport, and deliver all the goods and services required by consumers. But what to produce, where to deliver it, etc.—those are decisions that can be made wisely only if consumers are informed of the relative costs of producing various commodities and if firms are informed of the relative prices that consumers are willing to pay. It is the entire purpose of markets to transmit this information, and they can quite properly be judged by the accuracy and promptness with which they do so.

Competition transmits economic information faithfully. Each firm, under the impetus of profit-seeking, produces to the point where marginal cost equals price. The prices paid by consumers then measure the costs of the resources required to produce the goods they buy. If the price of any competitive good is so high that consumers are induced to substitute other products for it, the resources are released to produce those other products. Knowing the value of the goods that must be foregone to produce the things he buys—knowing, that is, the opportunity costs of his purchases—the consumer, by allocating his personal budget, can guide the producers to allocate the national resource budget in the way that satisfies him best.

The short-run adjustment will conduce to the best disposition of resources, including available plant and it will simultaneously point out the industries where plant expansion is needed most. For profits will be greatest where short-run marginal costs most exceed average costs, and those excesses will indicate precisely the industries wherein more and/or larger plants will be of greatest economic benefit in reducing marginal costs toward long-run average costs. In more concrete terms, a large excess of marginal costs over average costs indicates that labor and raw materials are being expended to overcome deficiencies in the available plant.

Monopoly and oligopoly, in their different ways, block the transmission of **110** the sort of information we have been discussing. In neither is the price of the product likely to be equal to its marginal cost: the monopolist does not wish it so, the oligopolist is too rigid to keep it so. And in neither does the level of profits automatically signal and induce the appropriate level of investment. We saw that in competitive markets new investment takes place until extraordinary profits are competed away, but this is not an outcome that holds much appeal for monopolists or oligopolists. Though they invest, they stop far short of that, and the entrenched positions of the established firms deter investment on the part of newcomers.

Regulation of monopoly is a partial cure for its defects. But the judgment of government authorities, especially when contested by the powerful companies they are charged with regulating, is a poor substitute for a sensitive market mechanism. Regulation brings prices into better accord with costs than they otherwise might be, but it also introduces rigidities that have something in common with those characteristic of oligopolies. Antitrust measures tend to produce oligopoly rather than competition.

Oligopolies suffer from being peculiarly rigid and unresponsive to market conditions. They also are practically compelled to dissipate economic resources in advertising [19] and in meretricious variations in product characteristics. And there is yet another objectionable side to oligopoly. Oligopoly induces advertising, and the function of advertising is to make consumers want the products advertised. But if the purpose of economic effort is to satisfy consumers' desires, what can be said in favor of a market form that makes consumers desire what the firms produce? What can we say for a form that makes people want to smoke in spite of the pleas of physicians? The answers to these and other critical questions like them deserve your attention. Unfortunately, we cannot explore them here.[20]

No effective means for regulating oligopolies have been devised—and it would be unreasonable to expect oligopolists to behave other than as they do; the system of rewards and punishments will tolerate nothing else of them.

The prevalence of monopoly and oligopoly is a serious defect in the free-market system of organizing economic activity. This system works best in its original environment of small-scale producers, and is less well adapted to controlling and guiding the industrial giants who have developed to take advantage of mass production and mass merchandising.

[19] The total bill for advertising has been estimated at around $12 billion a year, amounting to about 5 per cent of the value of the products advertised.

[20] For a trenchant development of this theme, see J. Kenneth Galbraith, *The Affluent Society* (Boston: Houghton Mifflin, 1958).

Marginal Revenue, Elasticity

and Monopolist's Profits

We shall develop the algebraic relationship between elasticity of demand and monopolist's profits, using the same general notation as in the appendix to Chapter 3. Let p be the price at which x units can be sold, and $p - \Delta p$ be the price at which $x + 1$ units can be sold. Then the total revenue when x units are sold is xp, and the total revenue when $x + 1$ units are sold is $(x + 1)(p - \Delta p)$. Marginal revenue when x units are sold is therefore by definition

$$\text{MR}(x) = (x + 1)(p - \Delta p) - xp$$
$$= p - x\Delta p - \Delta p$$
$$= p(1 \cdot - \frac{x}{p}\Delta p) - \Delta p$$

The second term is a negligible quantity in comparison with the first, and will be ignored. If we write $\Delta x = 1$, for the sake of symmetry, we then have

$$\text{MR}(x) = p\left(1 - \frac{x\Delta p}{p\Delta x}\right)$$

Let us denote the elasticity by the Greek letter *eta, η*. It is defined as *the ratio of the percentage change in the quantity demanded to the percentage change in price,* or

$$\eta = \frac{p\Delta x}{x\Delta p}$$

—which is the reciprocal of the fraction in the formula for marginal revenue. Hence marginal revenue, price, and elasticity are connected by the relationship

$$\text{MR}(x) = p\left(1 - \frac{1}{\eta}\right)$$

Solving this equation for $1/\eta$, we obtain

$$\frac{1}{\eta} = \frac{p - \text{MR}}{p} = \frac{p - \text{MC}}{p}$$

—as stated in the text.

Economic Efficiency

CHAPTER SEVEN

We come now to the crux of our discussion: the social function of prices and markets. In the preceding chapters we have taken up many details of economic organization—supply curves, the behavior of production costs, the logic of consumers' choices, and many others—because the mastering of details is the difference between reasoned understanding and bland acceptance. But such a thicket of technicalities tends to obscure the basic fact that the economic system is merely a device to aid in the making and carrying out of certain social decisions; and so in this chapter we shall concentrate on this central purpose of economic organization. First we shall lay down some general criteria expressing how an economic system should perform. Then we shall examine how a system organized around private firms and markets meets these criteria, and where such a system is likely to fall short. Though as we go along there may be a number of details still to be introduced on this point or that, we shall try to keep the big picture in mind throughout.

Our concern is with social decisions. Any decision is a choice among alternatives. Social decisions can be distinguished from technical decisions on the basis of the criteria used to evaluate the alternatives. A technical decision is one whose alternatives can be rated objectively according to the amount they contribute to attaining some single, well-defined goal. For example, if a river is to be dammed as cheaply as possible, the selection of the site at which construction cost is lowest is a technical decision. On the other hand, a social decision is one whose alternatives affect the attainment of a number of different goals, so that the choice among alternatives depends on the relative importance of those goals.

113

There is no purely objective way to rate the alternatives in a social decision. For example, if the cheapest site for the dam is also the one most destructive of scenery, and if scenery has social value, then a social decision is involved in the site selection. A single consumer's division of his budget among commodities is a social decision, according to this definition. Every decision that affects a number of people is a social decision, since the well-being of every individual is a distinguishable goal.

The essence of a social decision is that it impinges on a number of goals which are likely to conflict. If several people participate in the decision, they need some mode for expressing the relative importance they attach to the different goals. The thesis of this chapter, and even of this book, is that prices frequently fill this need. For this reason, prices have been called "coefficients of social choice." When prices are applicable, we have an economic decision. Economic decisions are easier than other types of social decisions simply because they benefit from this peculiarly efficient method for expressing and communicating individual preferences.

The circumstances in which prices are helpful in arriving at social decisions are complicated; indeed, it will take most of this chapter to explore them. But one aspect is clear at the outset: a price does not pertain to a social goal, but to an instrument for attaining it, called a *commodity*. This brings us back to the concept of opportunity cost: the price of a commodity measures its potential contribution to the attainment of the different goals to which it is applicable. A commodity should not be used for any purpose unless its contribution to the purpose is at least as important as its potential contribution to other social objectives, as indicated by its price. In this way, reference to prices can allocate commodities to the uses in which they make the greatest social contribution.

This, in essence, is the social function of our system of prices and markets. Now let us see how markets operate to fulfill this purpose. We start by stating some social criteria for the proper allocation of commodities.

THE THREE ASPECTS OF EFFICIENCY

At long last we are ready to confront the problem of allocation in an economy. The underlying principle is that no resource or other commodity should be used in any way if there is another use for it of greater social value. This is a very broad principle, which can usefully be divided into three parts: efficiency in distribution, efficiency in production, and consumers' sovereignty.

Efficiency in distribution means that the goods produced in the economy should be distributed to the consumers who want them. If things work out so that Mrs. Jones (who likes coffee) gets tea, and Mrs. O'Grady (who loves tea) gets coffee, the economy is not performing well in this respect. All systems of rationing, for instance, get low marks for distributional efficiency.

Efficiency in production means that as much should be produced of every desirable good as the available resources and technical knowledge permit, in light of the output of all the other desirable goods. A failure in this regard occurs whenever it is technically possible to increase the output of some commodity without reducing the output of any other.

Consumer sovereignty means that the goods produced should be the ones that the consumers want. When Henry Ford exclaimed that his customers could have any color car they liked, provided it was black, he was violating the standard of consumer sovereignty. Rationing systems do badly by this standard, too.

To produce goods and services in accordance with these three standards is the main task of an economy. We shall now look into each of them a bit more closely, in the order listed.

Efficiency in Distribution

An efficiently operating economy should distribute its products among consumers so that no one is forced to take one commodity when he prefers a different one that is also available. In other words, after the commodities have been allocated among consumers, there should not remain any way to reallocate them that would make some consumers better off without harming any other consumers.

This aspect of economic efficiency centers around the familiar concept of consumers' marginal rates of substitution. Think of any two commodities and suppose that there are two consumers in the economy who have different marginal rates of substitution between them. Then these two commodities could be reallocated so as to make both of those consumers better off without affecting anyone else. When any such easy opportunity for improving well-being remains, the current division of commodities among consumers cannot be fully efficient.

The argument behind these assertions is an extension of the reasoning of Chapter 5. Suppose that two members of the economy, Mrs. White and Mrs. Gray, have different marginal rates of substitution between some two commodities—say bread and wine. To be specific, suppose that Mrs. White's MRS(bread for wine) is 2 and that Mrs. Gray's is 3. Then Mrs. White would remain on the same indifference curve if she exchanged two loaves of bread for one pint of wine, or one pint of wine for two loaves of bread. And therefore she would move to a higher indifference curve if she exchanged one pint of her wine for 2½ loaves of Mrs. Gray's bread.

Mrs. Gray would also benefit from that exchange. She remains on the same indifference curve if she exchanges three loaves of bread for one pint of wine, and gains if she receives a pint of wine in return for only 2½ loaves. Therefore, an allocation of bread and wine to consumers is not fully efficient if it leaves a Mrs. White and a Mrs. Gray in the situation described, where a mutually advantageous opportunity for exchange still remains. Such an opportunity will remain if there is any pair of consumers who have different marginal rates of substitution between any pair of commodities, as we have just seen. We conclude, therefore, that:

> Efficient distribution of commodities requires that all consumers have the same marginal rate of substitution between every pair of commodities.

Notice that if all consumers buy their commodities at the same prices, their marginal rates of substitution will be equated automatically. For we saw in our study of consumption that each consumer chooses the quantities of different commodities so that his marginal rate of substitution between every pair of commodities is equal to the ratio of their prices. The allocation of commodities by consumer **115** choice on free markets, accordingly, achieves this kind of efficiency; it is very hard to attain otherwise.

The second main task of an economy is to produce the maximum possible output. Of course, the output of any single commodity can always be increased by shifting to it resources and efforts that are being used to produce other commodities—but that is not what this criterion means. It means that as much of each commodity should be produced as is possible without reducing the output of any other commodity. This is no mean feat in a varied and complicated economy, but the problem exists when there are as few as two commodities clamoring for the available resources, and it can be seen most clearly in that context.

To set forth the problem in its starkest form, let us think of Robinson Crusoe alone on his island. And let us from the first understand that Robinson Crusoe is only a piece of pedagogical scaffolding; the name is a code for any society, no matter how populous, that has well-defined, uniform objectives. (It happens that there are no such societies, except for Crusoe himself, but working out the economic principles for a one-man society is a large first step toward working out the principles for real societies. That is why we study Crusoe.)

The problem we give Crusoe can be stated very briefly. Everything he wants is available on his island in abundant supply, save only bread and wine. These he must produce if he wants them, and he does. All that he needs to produce bread and wine is land, of which he has, say, 100 acres. He can plant all 100 to wheat, but will then have no wine. Or he can plant all to vines and have no bread. Or, what is likely to be most sensible, he can divide the land between the two crops in any proportion he chooses, and have some of each.

Now think back to our study of consumption. For all that has been said so far, Crusoe, dividing his land between two crops, is in exactly the same position as a consumer dividing his budget between two commodities. The same principles would seem to apply, and we shall see that, with a slight modification, they do. The need for modification rises because Crusoe is also a producer, so that the principles of production, discussed in Chapters 3 and 4, must also apply to him. The crucial difference between consumers' and producers' choices is that when a consumer spends an additional dollar on a commodity, he receives an additional dollar's worth, but when a producer spends an additional dollar on a factor of production, he obtains a smaller increase in output than before, because of diminishing marginal productivity. Crusoe, too, must face this problem, but not in the familiar form because, being an isolate, he has no dollars-and-cents costs.

It is not hard to see that, in a sense, we have gotten down to the bare fundamentals—to the real phenomena that stand behind dollars and cents. Now we have to specify in some detail Crusoe's problem as a producer. This is done in Table 7-1, where it is assumed that Crusoe's 100 acres are divided into six classes of land. Some of this land is level and best suited for wheat (Types V and VI). Some is hilly and best adapted to wines (Types I and II). And there are graduations in between, as shown. These are all the production data we need.

Now we can see the decisions that Crusoe has to make. Essentially, they are two:

1. He must decide how much of each commodity to produce. But he cannot do this in a vacuum; he must take account of the fact that the more he produces of

one, the less he can have of the other. This decision is a strictly economic one. It depends on his preferences, and relates, indeed, to our third aspect of efficiency, consumers' sovereignty.

2. Whichever combination of outputs he selects, he must decide which land to use for each crop. This is a strictly technological problem. Preferences have nothing to do with it; it depends only on allocating the different classes of land so as to obtain the largest possible crops over-all.

These two decisions are closely intertwined. For one thing, if the technological decision is made unwisely, Crusoe the consumer will have to be content with a smaller total output than is really necessary. Besides, as we shall see, the analysis of the technological decision provides information about the marginal costs of wheat and wine that is useful in making the economic decision. The technological decision is our present concern.

Technical Decisions; Production Possibility Frontier. The technical conditions of production, specified in Table 7-1, determine the range of choice open to Crusoe, the range within which he must finally make his economic decision. At one extreme, if he devotes all his land to wheat, he can produce 1,125 bushels, as shown in the next-to-last column. This same possibility is shown in Fig. 7-1, as the right-hand end of the broken-line curve there drawn. Now suppose that Crusoe would like to have 100 gallons of wine. Then he faces his first, and most critical, technological decision: which type of land to use. He might be tempted at first to use land of Type II, which has the largest output of wine per acre. But that would be wrong. To produce 100 gallons of wine on Type II land would require 2½ acres, enough to grow 15 bushels of wheat. But on Type I land, 100 gallons of wine require 3⅓ acres on which only 10 bushels of wheat can be grown. Clearly he has to sacrifice fewer bushels of wheat for his 100 gallons of wine if he uses Type I land than if he uses Type II.

The general principle here at work is one of the most important and pervasive principles of production economics, known as the principle of *comparative ad-*

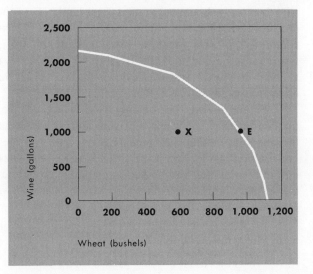

FIG 7-1 The production possibility frontier for Crusoe's island shows all efficient combinations of outputs.

Table 7-1   ROBINSON CRUSOE'S PRODUCTION POSSIBILITIES

Class of Land	Acres	Output per Acre Wheat (bushels)	Wine (gallons)	Output Ratio Wheat/ Wine	Potential Output Wheat (bushels)	Wine (gallons)
I	10	3	30	0.10	30	300
II	10	6	40	0.15	60	400
III	20	9	30	0.30	180	600
IV	25	12	20	0.60	300	500
V	25	15	10	1.50	375	250
VI	10	18	5	3.60	180	50
Total	100				1,125	2,100

Note: By world standards this is very poor land and especially unfitted for wine production.

vantage. It applies whenever a decision can be made about which factors to use in producing a given commodity, and it provides us with this very commonsensical rule: *Always use the factors that are least productive in alternative applications in comparison with their productivity for the commodity desired.*

Let us make the required comparison for Type I and Type II land. The marginal productivity [1] of Type I land is 3 bushels per acre when used to produce wheat, and 30 gallons per acre when used for wine. Thus, its marginal productivity in wheat is one-tenth of its marginal productivity when used for wine (see the fifth column of the table). The same comparison for Type II land shows that its wheat productivity is about one-seventh of its wine productivity (ignoring units of measurement, which cancel out). So Type I land is relatively less productive of wheat than Type II land, and should be used for producing the 100 gallons of wine. In that way, less wheat will have to be sacrificed to obtain the wine than would be possible with any other choice.

The comparative advantage rule is just another version of the opportunity cost principle. The opportunity cost of a gallon of wine is the amount of wheat that has to be foregone in order to produce it. The comparative advantage rule tells us to produce the wine in such a way that this sacrifice of wheat, or opportunity cost, is as small as possible. This establishes that when the production of wine begins, it should begin on Type I land, where the number of bushels of wheat sacrificed per gallon of wine produced is lowest. When all the Type I land has been committed to wine (that is, when more than 300 gallons of wine are desired), resort must be had to Type II land, which has the next highest comparative advantage in wheat. And so on down the list, which has been arranged in order of comparative advantage in wine production.

Figure 7-1 has been constructed in accordance with this principle. It shows the combinations of wheat and wine output that result when the first 300 gallons of wine (or fraction thereof) are produced on Type I land, the next 400 gallons (or fraction thereof) on Type II land, and so on. Accordingly, it shows the greatest output of wine that can be had in conjunction with any given output of wheat and, conversely, the greatest output of wheat attainable with any given output of wine. It shows, in short, the complete menu of choice.

To drive things home: suppose that the principle of comparative advantage were violated—what then? Suppose, say, that 950 gallons of wine were desired

[1] And also average productivity, as it happens.

and that they were grown on land of the even-numbered types. Then 585 bushels of wheat would be grown on the land of odd-numbered types, resulting in the output shown by point X in Fig. 7-1. Clearly that is an inefficient allocation, since point E shows that 960 bushels of wheat can be had in conjunction with 950 gallons of wine with a proper allocation of the land.

The broken-line curve in Fig. 7-1 is known as the *production possibility frontier*.

> The production possibility frontier shows the greatest amount of one commodity that can be produced in conjunction with any prescribed amounts of all the other commodities in the economy.

This production possibility frontier is obviously of the greatest importance to Robinson Crusoe. It tells him what he can afford, just as the ordinary budget line tells the consumer what he can afford. In exactly the same way, the vastly more complicated production possibility frontier of a real economy is of the greatest importance to the members of that economy. It prescribes the complete range of choice of consumption goods open to the members of that economy.

Two geometrical characteristics of the production possibility frontier are noteworthy. First, it curves downward as we move to the right; in technical language, it is concave.[2] This is a direct consequence of the principle of comparative advantage. Starting at the left-hand end (no wheat produced), the first land to be converted to wheat will have a comparative advantage in wheat—i.e., will require the smallest reduction in wine output per bushel of wheat produced. When all of this land has been converted, then land where the sacrifice in wine is somewhat higher will have to be used, making the curve steeper. And so it will go.

What is true on Crusoe's island is true in general. The resources used to produce any commodity in an efficient economy will be those whose use entails the smallest sacrifice possible of other commodities. As the output of any commodity is increased, resources less well adapted to it will have to be drawn in, and the sacrifice of other commodities will increase. This produces the curvature shown. It also accounts for the cost curves studied in Chapter 3.

The second noteworthy property of the production possibility frontier is that its slope at any output point has an evident economic meaning. It is the number of gallons of wine that must be foregone in order to obtain one more bushel of wheat. This ratio is known as the *marginal rate of transformation* of wine into wheat.

> The marginal rate of transformation of wine into wheat at any point of the production possibility frontier, denoted MRT (wine for wheat), is the number of units of wine that have to be given up in order to produce one additional unit of wheat.

[2] The production possibility frontier in Fig. 7-1 is made up of six line segments because we distinguished six qualities of land. If we had assumed that there were a great many different types of land, the line segments would have been vastly more numerous and shorter, so that the frontier would be indistinguishable from a smooth curve. The curve would remain concave, however, looking generally like an isoquant turned upside-down.

There is no way to say for sure whether the production possibility frontiers of real economies are more like smooth curves or more like broken-line curves. Economists use both versions, depending on which is the more convenient for a particular problem. The smooth frontier is the traditional version, dating back to Ricardo's day, but the broken-line type is currently enjoying a vogue because the associated mathematics, called *linear programing*, has proved remarkably fruitful in business and economic applications.

The name is a happy one, though it suggests that there is some mystical alchemy for transforming wine into wheat. Wine can indeed be transformed into wheat in an economy—not, to be sure, after it is fermented, but before the vines are planted, by the unmystical economic method of redirecting resources from wine to wheat production. We shall use the MRT (wine for wheat) in the next section.

All of this ought to sound vaguely familiar. Our new concepts of the production possibility frontier and the marginal rate of transformation are merely restatements, at a more fundamental level, of the analysis of the firm in Chapters 3 and 4. The individual businessman decides which resources to use on the basis of their prices; he chooses the cheapest possible combination of resources with which to produce his output. But the prices of factors of production are merely reflections of their productivities in different employments. When there are no prices, the marginal productivities of factors in different employments have to be compared in physical units, as we have just done, but the principle is the same no matter which units are used for the comparisons.

We have now solved the problem of efficient production on Crusoe's island. He will allocate his land between wheat and wine so as to attain one of the output points on his production possibility frontier. More generally:

> An efficient economic system will allocate resources so as to obtain outputs on its production possibility frontier (rather than wastefully small outputs such as point X).

Consumer Sovereignty

Consumer sovereignty exists in an economy when that economy is responsive to consumers' desires; that is to say, when that economy does not devote resources to producing any good if those resources could have been used to produce something that consumers would have preferred. This is the standard that monopolies violate. It entails that producers should somehow know which commodities consumers want most, and that consumers, on their part, should know enough about the conditions of production so that they can formulate realistic demands.

On Crusoe's island, where producer and consumer are one, the problem is trivially simple, and yet we can learn something from it. We have already seen how Crusoe can attain any of the points on his production possibility frontier. Now we ask which point he should select.

Once Crusoe has determined his production possibility frontier he behaves like a consumer except that he has a production possibility frontier instead of a budget line. This is shown in Fig. 7-2, where a few of Crusoe's indifference curves between wheat and wine are superimposed on the graph of the production possibility frontier. He selects point *P,* where the frontier touches the highest possible indifference curve. All other points on the frontier are on lower indifference curves (that is, they are less desirable). He does not have to be content with any point below the frontier, and he cannot attain any point above it. Point *P* is the best output combination he can attain, as evaluated by Crusoe's own preferences and desires.

The essential fact to notice in Fig. 7-2 is that at the optimum point the frontier is tangent to the relevant indifference curve (that is, their slopes are equal). The slope of the indifference curve, we know, is the marginal rate of substitution between the two commodities; the slope of the production possibility frontier is their marginal rate of transformation. Hence:

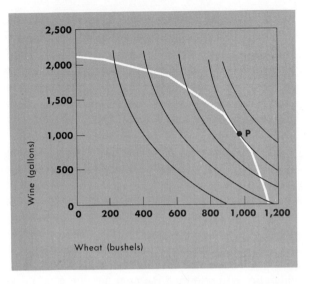

FIG 7-2 The best point on the production possibility frontier is where it is tangent to the highest possible indifference curve.

Wine (gallons)

Wheat (bushels)

The optimal output for a one-consumer economy occurs at the point where the economy's marginal rate of transformation between any two commodities is equal to the consumer's marginal rate of substitution between them.

That solves the problem for Robinson Crusoe—but not, unfortunately, for any economy with more than one member. Any economy, no matter how populous, has a production possibility frontier and attains it when operating efficiently. What a populous economy lacks is a well-defined set of indifference curves such as the ones we used to resolve Crusoe's final choice in Fig. 7-2. This difficulty obtrudes itself even when there are only two members in the economy.

To see our way into this problem, let us provide Crusoe with a companion, not Man Friday but a doughty equal named Smith. Then Crusoe and Smith have to agree on a point on the production possibility frontier, and on a division between them of the amounts of the two crops corresponding to that point. These are two distinct decisions involving different social issues. We shall deal with them separately, taking up first the question of how to divide the crops corresponding to any selected point on the production possibility frontier.

To this end, suppose that an output point such as point P in Fig. 7-2 has been selected. A thousand gallons of wine plus 945 bushels of wheat are available to be shared between Crusoe and Smith. The only principle that we have to go on is that the wheat and wine should be shared in such a way that Crusoe and Smith have the same marginal rate of substitution between the two commodities. But this principle is not sufficient to determine the division of the crops; it can be satisfied in too many different ways. A famous diagram, called a *box diagram,* will help us to visualize the problem and its social implications.

The box diagram is based on the indifference curve diagrams introduced in Chapter 5. Figure 7-3 shows a few of Crusoe's indifference curves between wheat and wine. The only new feature is that the indifference curves are enclosed in a box whose dimensions are the total amounts of the commodities to be divided. Each point in the box therefore shows the quantities assigned to Crusoe, in the conventional way, and also the quantities left over to be assigned to Smith. According to point *A*, for example, Crusoe gets 480 bushels of wheat and 400 gallons of wine. Smith gets the remainder: 465 bushels of wheat and 600 gallons of wine, as can be read off the two new axes in the diagram. Crusoe's indifference curves, as shown, indicate how he rates different possible divisions of the two crops. He prefers *B* to *A* and *A* to *C*. Smith's preferences among divisions cannot be told from Fig. 7-3, but we can take care of that by adding some of Smith's indifference curves to the diagram. This is done in Fig. 7-4. Smith's curves may look a bit peculiar in that diagram, but if you turn the page upside down you will see that they form a perfectly normal indifference curve diagram referred to as Smith's *O*, *O* point. Now we can see that Smith's ranking of divisions *A*, *B*, *C* is just the opposite of Crusoe's.

The divisions that correspond to points at which one of Smith's indifference curves is tangent to one of Crusoe's are of special importance. To emphasize them, the curve *FYE*, called the *contract curve,* is drawn through all such points. For, consider any point (such as point *A*) not on the contract curve: like every other point, it lies on one of Crusoe's indifference curves. As we move along that indifference curve toward the contract curve at *Y*, we pass through a succession of

FIG 7-3 Each point in a box diagram specifies one way of dividing given amounts of two commodities between two consumers.

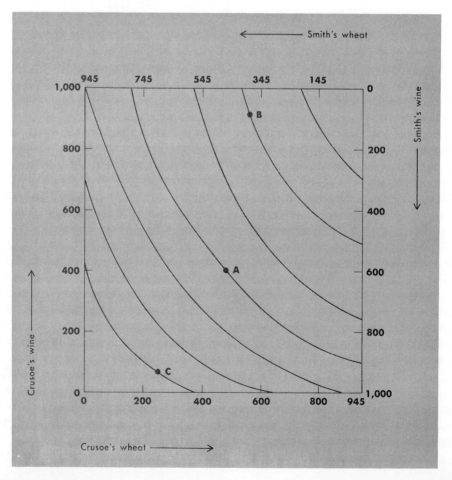
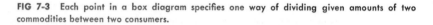

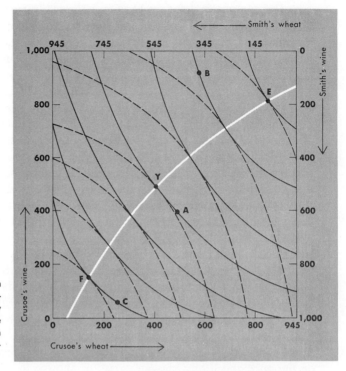

FIG 7-4 The indifference curves in the box diagram show the preferences of both consumers. Every point at which two indifference curves are tangent represents an efficient distribution of the commodities between the consumers.

points representing divisions that are only equally satisfactory from Crusoe's point of view, but are increasingly good according to Smith's scale of preferences. But at Y we reach the highest indifference curve for Smith that intersects the given indifference curve for Crusoe. We cannot find any reallocation taking Y as a point of departure that benefits Smith without harming Crusoe—and this is the fundamental characteristic of the contract curve. Any division *off* the contract curve can be improved from the viewpoints of both Crusoe and Smith; no division *on* it can be.

There is nothing surprising about all this when we remember that the slope of an indifference curve is the graphic representation of the consumer's marginal rate of substitution between the commodities. On the contract curve, where Smith's and Crusoe's indifference curves are tangent, the two men have the same marginal rate of substitution between the commodities, and we have already found this to be a condition for an efficient distribution of the commodities between them. The trouble is that there are so many such points; FYE is full of them.

So the situation is this: the principle of equating marginal rates of substitution tells us to divide the wheat and wine between Crusoe and Smith according to some point on the contract curve, but it doesn't tell us which point. However, a glance at the box diagram shows what is involved in a choice among points on the contract curve. As we move along the curve from F toward E, we move through successively higher indifference curves for Crusoe, and lower ones for Smith. In other words, as we move in that direction, Crusoe gets richer at Smith's expense. The choice we are now considering is the choice of income distribution, one of the most serious and contentious questions in any society. Indeed, Crusoe and Smith are likely to argue vehemently about which point to choose on FYE.

Although we cannot go into the question of income distribution until the next chapter, at this point we have to make two remarks about it. The first is that every society must have some rules and procedures for dividing its income among its members. The second is that whatever these rules and procedures may be, in the interest of economic efficiency they should permit a division of commodities that lies on the contract curve.

We have answered as fully as we can here the first question we posed: how Crusoe and Smith should divide the crops resulting from any point on the production possibility frontier. The rules of their society must specify a distribution of income corresponding to each such point. If Crusoe and Smith decide to produce at point *P,* that decision will determine the quantities of the crops to be divided and the dimensions of the box diagram. The rule of income distribution will then settle which point on the contract curve will be adopted. More than that: since Crusoe and Smith have the same MRS (wine for wheat) at every point on the contract curve, though this marginal rate of substitution is likely to be different at different points, the output decision plus the rule determine an MRS (wine for wheat) common to both, or all, members of the society.

Now we can deal with the second question: which point to select on the production possibility frontier. Another graph will be helpful here: in Fig. 7-5 the same production productivity frontier is reproduced, with a slight change. We now drop the assumption that there are only six classes of land, in favor of the more realistic view that there is a very large number. Then the production productivity frontier will consist of a very large number of very short segments, and will take on the appearance of a smooth curve, as shown. It will still be concave, for the principle of comparative advantage still applies. Each point on the frontier signifies certain outputs of the two commodities to which there corresponds a certain division between the claimants and, as we just saw, a certain communal marginal rate of substitution between wine and wheat. The marginal rate of substitution is represented graphically by a slope—specifically, by the common slope of the indifference curves on which the participants find themselves at that point. This slope at point *P* is indicated by the short line-segment drawn through that point.

Notice, now, that this slope is not the same as that of the production possibility

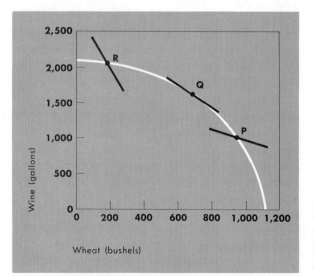

FIG 7-5 When there are several consumers, the best point on the production possibility frontier is the point where the slope of the frontier and the communal marginal rate of substitution are the same.

frontier at point P—i.e., the marginal rate of transformation there. Therefore, point P cannot be a good choice. For the slope of the communal MRS line, as we may call it, shows the number of gallons of wine that either member of the community would require to recompense him for a one-bushel reduction is his quota of wheat, in accordance with his indifference curve. The slope of the production possibility curve shows the number of gallons of wine that can be obtained by reducing the output of wheat by one bushel. As shown, the increase in wine output is more than sufficient to compensate either member for a bushel reduction in his wheat allotment. So one member could be made better off, and the other not harmed, if a production point were selected at which one bushel less of wheat was grown and MRT(wine for wheat) more gallons of wine. Point P is not a good selection on the production possibility frontier.

But now consider point Q, where it happens that the communal marginal rate of substitution is equal to the marginal rate of transformation. There, a small diminution in wheat output will not permit a large enough increase in wine production to promote either member to a higher indifference curve. Similarly, the sacrifice in wine output required to obtain an additional bushel of wheat is not large enough to compensate either member for a bushel reduction in his wheat allotment. If point Q is selected, there is no way to increase the well-being of either member without decreasing that of the other. Thus point Q may well be a good production point.

Must there necessarily be a point such as Q, where the marginal rate of transformation is equal to the communal marginal rate of substitution? We would need an elaborate analysis to answer this question rigorously, including a detailed specification of the rules of income distribution, but it seems very plausible that there should be such a point if communal behavior is at all like individual behavior. At a point such as R, wine is very plentiful in proportion to wheat. At such a production point for the community most consumers, if not all, will be allotted a great deal of wine in proportion to wheat and, in accordance with their individual indifference curves, such consumers will have high MRS(wine for wheat). Since the communal marginal rate of substitution reflects individual ones, it will be likely to be high also, as illustrated by the steep communal MRS line. Note that at that same point the production possibility frontier is quite flat, indicating a low MRT(wine for wheat).

At point P, where wheat is plentiful in proportion to wine, the situation is just the opposite. It seems reasonable to believe that the two slopes, one representing preferences and the other production possibilities, will come together at some point intermediate between R and P. There the marginal rate of substitution and the marginal rate of transformation will be equal. Any such point will have the essential property that no reallocation of resources between the commodities will enable either consumer to reach a higher indifference curve.

At this point the requirements of consumer sovereignty are fulfilled. The consumers—all two of them—are as well satisfied as physical circumstances permit, in the sense that there is no way to move one of them to a higher indifference curve without moving another to a lower indifference curve. The importance of the distribution of income in determining the output point dictated by consumer sovereignty is worth emphasizing. The distribution of income determined the communal marginal rate of substitution. The output point responsive to consumer sovereignty is the one at which the marginal rate of transformation is equal to the communal marginal rate of substitution. Of course it follows that consumers do not share their sovereignty equally; the economy is most responsive to the tastes of the richer consumers.

MORE GENERAL CASES

Our previous reasoning applies, almost verbatim, if there are more than two consumers. We already know that no matter how many consumers there may be, distributional efficiency requires that the goods be allotted so that there exists a communal marginal rate of substitution between them, shared by all the consumers. If the economy is producing at a point on its production possibility frontier where the marginal rate of transformation is different from this communal marginal rate of substitution, then a slight movement along the frontier can promote at least one consumer to a higher indifference curve without harming any other. Furthermore, our reasoning extends to economies with any numbers of commodities, because we can think of holding the amounts of all commodities constant except for one pair. For the outputs of that pair to be in proper relation to each other, they must be such that the same old equality is satisfied; namely, such that the marginal rate of transformation of the members of that pair equals the communal marginal rate of substitution between them. You may not be sure that this comparison is always meaningful (for instance, that it is possible to "transform" wool into wedding rings without affecting the output of anything else, by redirecting resources in a real economy), but at bottom, all commodities in an integrated economy draw on a common pool of resources, so that these shifts, though complicated, can be made.[3]

It follows that, irrespective of the numbers of consumers and commodities in an economy:

> When an economy is operating efficiently, the marginal rate of transformation between any pair of commodities produced will be equal to the communal marginal rate of substitution between them.

When this condition is satisfied, the economy is operating in accordance with the principle of consumer sovereignty.

SUMMARY OF CONDITIONS
FOR ECONOMIC EFFICIENCY

Let us recapitulate the findings of this long but basic discussion of the requirements for economic efficiency. Three aspects of efficiency must all be attained, and each of them requires that a different kind of marginal equality be satisfied. They are:

[3] For example, some wool spinners may have to shift to spinning rayon, so that the rayon industry can substitute spinners for chemists (spinning more carefully fiber made under lower standards of quality control), thus releasing the chemists needed to supervise the refining of more gold. Even longer chains of substitutions may be required.

1. Efficiency in distribution—distributing the available output so as to satisfy consumers as well as possible. This requires that all consumers share a common marginal rate of substitution between every pair of commodities.
2. Efficiency in production—producing as much as possible of each good without sacrificing any other good. This requires that each resource be used in the employment for which it has a comparative advantage, or for which its marginal productivity is greatest in comparison with its marginal productivity in alternative employments.
3. Consumer sovereignty—using each resource to produce the commodities which consumers desire the most. This requires that the marginal rate of transformation between every pair of commodities equal the communal marginal rate of substitution between them.

These three conditions together characterize perfect economic efficiency— more efficiency than we have a right to expect of any functioning, complicated economy. If you think about them for a moment, you will see that they are very similar and rather peculiar. All three tests of efficiency are unanimity tests. Each says that an economy is falling short of perfect efficiency in one respect or another if all members of the economy agree that the results it is producing are less desirable than some other result that could also be attained. If the members of the economy disagree—if only a tiny minority dissents from the general opinion—our three criteria say nothing. In principle, then, an economy may score high marks on all these tests while displeasing, or even oppressing, the great majority of its members. In other words, these three criteria of efficiency are strictly economic tests of performance; they have nothing to do with social justice, improving the quality of life, or any consideration other than minimizing unambiguous waste—that is, avoiding any choice when another is possible that is better from everyone's point of view.

These criteria have been very carefully constructed over the generations with unanimity of mind. One of the hallmarks of a scientific statement is that it can gain the assent of all reasonable men who understand it. The three criteria and their logical implications are scientific by this standard, but at the cost of remaining mute about all the important issues of economic and social policy about which reasonable and informed men can disagree. However, these criteria do take us close to the limits of scientific economics, and it is remarkable that so much can be said within the stringent limitation of universal agreement.

A free market economy guided by competitive prices is remarkably well adapted to satisfy these three efficiency criteria. In the earlier chapters we saw, in bits and pieces, how producers and consumers react in a free market economy. Next we shall put those bits and pieces together to see how a free market system meets the triple challenge.

The Interplay of Markets

CHAPTER EIGHT

PRICES AND EFFICIENCY

Prices and Efficient Distribution

A free market distributes commodities among customers efficiently in the easiest conceivable way. Each consumer has a budget, which is really an undifferentiated claim upon the commodities in the economy. He can distribute this claim to suit himself among all the commodities he desires, buying them at prices that he cannot influence appreciably. He is best pleased when he purchases such quantities of commodities that his marginal rate of substitution between each pair equals the ratio of their prices. Since all consumers make their decisions in the light of the same prices, they all have the same marginal rate of substitution between every pair of commodities. The condition for distributional efficiency is satisfied forthwith.

Prices and Efficient Production

The preceding was the trivial aspect. Now let us turn to how prices operating through free markets lead firms to the achievement of productive efficiency, or, what is the same thing, how they guide the economy to some point on its production possibility frontier. Remarkably, they do this in spite of the fact that in a real economy the production possibility frontier is so complicated that no one really knows where it is.

Several mechanisms operate simultaneously to achieve this result, but we can get at the essence by reverting to Robinson

Crusoe's production problem. Remember that he had two commodities, and six factors (i.e., six types of land) to allocate among them. We can make this example more pertinent to our current interest by imagining that each type of land (or even each acre of land) is operated by a separate firm that doesn't know where the production possibility frontier is, and doesn't even care very much. All that any firm has to know is its own production possibilities *and* the prices of the two products. Suppose that the price of wine is $1 a gallon and of wheat $2 a bushel. Then, using the data of Table 7-1, Firm I, operating Type I land, can earn $30 on each acre it uses for wine, but only $6 on an acre used for wheat. Its decision is clear. Firm VI, operating Type VI land, on the other hand, earns $5 on each acre used for wine, and $36 on an acre of wheat land. Its decision is clear, too. In fact, at these prices, Types I, II, and III land will be used for wine, and Types IV, V, and VI for wheat. This allocation is on the production possibility frontier. No one has given a thought to the principle of comparative advantage, but everyone has obeyed its dictates.

If the prices of the products change, so will the allocation of the land, but the result will always be on the production possibility frontier. And any point on the frontier can be attained by the proper prices, which are prices in the ratio of the marginal rate of transformation at that point. For example, since Crusoe desires production at point P (Fig. 7-2) he should announce that he is willing to pay $1 for a bushel of wheat and 60¢ for a gallon of wine. Then Firms I, II, and III will offer him wine, Firms V and VI will offer wheat, and Firm IV won't care which it produces, and might as well split its land 50-50.[1]

The reason that prices work so handily is that they reflect opportunity costs. In a real economy, Type I land would rent for either $3p_b$ or $30\ p_v$ per acre, whichever is higher (p_b = price of wheat, p_v = price of wine), for that is what some competing firm would be willing to pay for its use. The owner of the land could not afford to use it for a purpose that yielded less than its opportunity cost.

So prices will certainly solve Crusoe's production problem for him. They will also solve far more complicated production problems, though Crusoe's island economy is much too simple to illustrate the subtlety and power of prices in this respect. We can indicate how prices work, however, by invoking some of the principles deduced in Chapter 4. Our argument depends on the following fact: If an economy has a price system and is producing the bundle of commodities that has the greatest possible aggregate value, then it is operating at a point on its production possibility frontier. This is true because, by the definition of "frontier," if it were not on its production possibility frontier, there would be some rearrangement of its production activities and its use of resources that would increase the output of some commodity without reducing the output of any other. But such a rearrangement would increase the aggregate value of output. It follows that maximizing the value of output at any set of prices is equivalent to attaining a point on the production possibility frontier. Which point on the frontier is attained depends on which prices are used.

---

[1] The indeterminacy encountered by Firm IV results from the long, flat line segments. It doesn't arise with a smooth production possibility frontier, as in Fig. 7-5, but the arithmetic there is not as transparent.

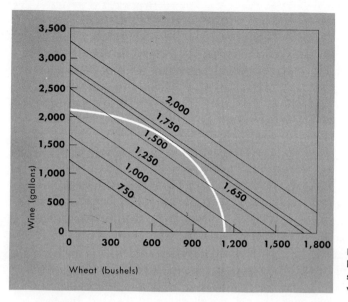

FIG 8-1 If there are prices, the best point on the production possibility frontier maximizes the total value of output.

The relationship between the value of output and the production possibility frontier is illustrated in Fig. 8-1. There, Robinson Crusoe's production possibility frontier is reproduced and some lines are superimposed, along each of which the value of output is constant at prices of $1 per bushel of wheat and 60¢ per gallon of wine.[2] The greatest possible value of output occurs where the production possibility frontier touches, and is tangent to, the line for combinations of outputs worth $1,650. If we had drawn constant-value lines for any other set of prices we should have obtained a similar result: the greatest possible value would correspond to some point on the production possibility frontier.

Now, when firms operate to maximize their profits at given prices, they simultaneously maximize the aggregate value of output of the economy. This is implied by the findings of Chapter 4. First, under the inducement of the market prices, each firm produces the output of greatest possible value with the resources it uses. When firms have done this, no rearrangement of resources within the firms will increase the aggregate value of the output of the economy. Second, we have to consider whether aggregate value could be increased by some reassignment of factors of production from one firm to another. Recall, now, that the wage or rental paid to any factor is equal to the value of its marginal product—that is, to the value of its contribution to the output of the firm that employs it. If some factor should be transferred from one firm to another, therefore, two things will happen. The value produced by the firm that loses the factor will fall by an amount equal to the wage or rental of the factor. At the same time, the value produced by the firm that gains the factor will increase by this same amount. These two changes cancel each other out, and the aggregate value of output produced by the economy will not increase.

In short, no reallocation of resources can increase the value of output of an economy if (a) each firm is maximizing its profit with reference to some set of

[2] The formula for these lines is:

$$1 \times \text{bushels of wheat} + .60 \times \text{gallons of wine} = \text{total value of output.}$$

prices, and (b) each factor of production is paid according to the value of its marginal product. This means, as we have seen, that under those circumstances the economy will be on its production possibility frontier. The operation of competitive markets tends to establish conditions (a) and (b), and therefore to guide the economy to some point on its production possibility frontier.[3]

We have now demonstrated that when all firms are in equilibrium, an economy made up of competitive markets will be at some point on its production possibility frontier. Which point will be arrived at depends on the prices. Figure 8-1 suggests, correctly, that it will be at the point where the marginal rate of transformation between any pair of commodities equals the ratio of their prices. This is where consumer sovereignty, the ultimate determinator of prices, enters the picture.

Prices and Consumer Sovereignty

The final task of an economy is to satisfy consumers as well as circumstances permit. No economy is rich enough to provide consumers with everything they want, but what we can demand of an economic system is that it not devote its resources to producing one thing when those same resources could be used to produce something else that consumers want more. A system in which production is responsive to freely adjusting competitive market prices answers this demand. We shall show that when market prices have adjusted so that the quantity supplied of every commodity equals the quantity demanded, the dictates of consumer sovereignty are being obeyed.

We can see this most clearly by observing how markets would operate in the two-commodity world. Suppose now that Crusoe's island has become populated by families, each of which owns some of the land and derives its income by selling the wine and wheat that it grows. Each family spends its income by buying wheat and wine at market prices. Even in this simple economy there are supply and demand curves to determine the prices of the two commodities. Let us look first at the supply curve for wheat. The supply of wheat depends on how much land is devoted to it and this, in turn, depends on the ratio of the price of wheat to the price of wine. In order to see how this supply responds to changes in the price of wheat we have, therefore, to assume some definite, fixed price for wine. Suppose that it is 60¢ a gallon. Then the supply curve for wheat can be calculated as follows.

Each acre of land will be used for wheat or wine, depending on which is the more profitable. Suppose that some particular acre can be used to produce y_b bushels of wheat or y_v gallons of wine, and that the price of wheat is p_b a bushel. Then that acre will be used for wheat if and only if $y_b p_b \geq .60 y_v$ or $y_v/y_b \leq p_b/.60$.

---

[3] This demonstration that competitive markets guide an economy toward its production possibility frontier makes no pretense of being rigorous. To mention just one defect: we showed that no single transfer of resources could increase the value of the economy's output, and implied that therefore no sequence or combination of transfers could do so. But this implication, itself, requires proof. The proof would depend on the properties of the isoquant diagrams and the production functions described in Chapter 4.

All really adequate treatments of the relationship between prices and productive efficiency are very difficult. For a somewhat fuller discussion, see Robert Dorfman, *The Price System*, in this Series, Chapter 5. For a still more extensive discussion, which may be understandable, see R. Dorfman, P. A. Samuelson, and R. M. Solow, *Linear Programming and Economic Analysis*, Chapter 13.

Furthermore, the borderline acres are those for which equality applies in this expression. But the ratio of the yields on the borderline acres is the marginal rate of transformation of wine into wheat and, accordingly, is the slope of the production possibility frontier at the output corresponding to this price. We can therefore read the supply of wheat corresponding to any price right off the production possibility frontier (Fig. 7-5). For example, if the price of wheat is $1 a bushel, the marginal rate of transformation of wine into wheat will be $1:.60 = 1.67$. The production possibility frontier has this slope when 690 bushels of wheat are produced. Accordingly, 690 bushels are supplied at a price of $1 a bushel. This is one of the points on the supply curve for wheat. Other points can be read off the production possibility frontier in the same way. The entire supply curve, so derived, is shown in Fig. 8-2.

If we wished to derive a demand curve for wheat analogously from fundamentals, we should have to start our reasoning with the indifference curve diagrams of the individual consumers and the rules for the distribution of income among them. In the absence of these data, a demand curve has been drawn on Fig. 8-2 arbitrarily. The two curves cross at the equilibrium point for the wheat market: a price of $1 a bushel and a quantity of 690 bushels.

The derivation of the supply curve showed that at an output of 690 bushels the marginal rate of transformation of wine into wheat was $1:0.60$; i.e., the reciprocal of the ratio of the prices. At those prices each consumer will divide his budget between wine and wheat so that his marginal rate of substitution of wine for wheat will also be $1:0.60$. But the demand curve shows that when the consumers have adjusted their budgets so as to attain this marginal rate of substitution, they will be demanding 690 bushels. Thus the output that clears the wheat market also

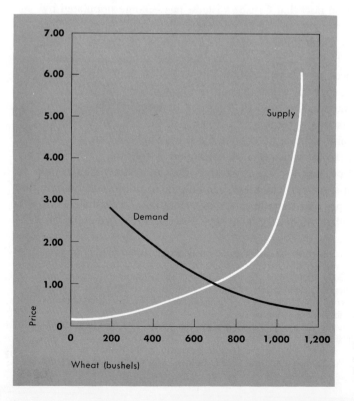

FIG 8-2 Supply and demand curves are significant, even in a two-commodity economy.

and necessarily equates the marginal rate of transformation to the marginal rate of substitution for each consumer.

In spite of the complications introduced by having many consumers deal indirectly with many producers through purchase and sale on a market, this is very much like the equilibrium attained when Robinson Crusoe was the sole consumer. Then (Fig. 7-2), equilibrium was attained where the production possibility frontier had the same slope as the highest indifference curve Crusoe could reach. Now, equilibrium is attained where the production possibility frontier has the same slope as each consumer's highest attainable indifference curve. In both cases it is physically impossible to produce enough wheat by giving up wine (or enough wine by giving up wheat) to promote any consumer to a higher indifference curve.

The main difference between the two cases is that when Crusoe was alone, the information about the production possibility frontier and the indifference curve was all contained in a single head. When there are numerous producers and consumers, each producer knows only his own production possibilities, each consumer knows only his own preferences, and they communicate with each other only by their responses to different prices. But this indirect communication is enough to satisfy the consumers as well as the production possibilities permit.

We mustn't forget about the wine. Given that prices of $1 a bushel for wheat and 60¢ a gallon for wine clear the wheat market, do they do the same for wine? They must, by simple arithmetic. The production possibility frontier tells us that when 690 bushels of wheat are produced (worth $690) the output of wine will be 1,600 gallons (worth $960, at 60¢ a gallon). Since everything produced in the economy belongs to some member of it, the total income of the economy will be $1,650. Finally, if consumers are willing to spend $690 on wheat, as the demand curve says they are, they will have $960 left over, which is just enough to buy the total output of wine. The prices that clear either market clear the other one also.

This reasoning is perfectly general. It depends on the fact that production and earning income are two aspects of the same activity. The value of everything produced (at any prices whatever) is a component of somebody's income, and there is no way to earn income except by participating in production. Hence the total value produced and the total income earned in an economy are the same, and there is always just enough income to buy the entire output. It follows that in an economy that produces 100,000 different commodities, a set of prices that clears the markets for 99,999 of them will leave just enough money over to clear the remaining market.[4]

We find, therefore, that when there are only two commodities there will be

---

[4] The balance between total incomes and the total value of output is more complicated in real economies than in this one. International trade, in which members of one economy sell to and buy from members of others, introduces new considerations. The operations of governments, which collect taxes and disburse subsidies and benefits, also complicate the balance. But the most serious problem we have ignored is the problem of hoarding: some consumers may choose to spend less than their entire incomes, desiring to put aside some money for later use. When that happens it may be impossible for all markets to clear simultaneously at any set of prices. This is called "macroeconomic disequilibrium"—disequilibrium not specific to any market but relating to the total values of goods produced and demanded. It is analyzed elsewhere in this Series by C. L. Schultze in *National Income Analysis*, 2nd ed., and J. S. Duesenberry in *Money and Credit: Impact and Control*, 2nd ed.

some prices that clear the markets for both of them, and that those prices will induce a pattern of production that is obedient to consumers' sovereignty. When there are more commodities life is more complicated, but precisely the same mechanism is at work. Suppose that bread is one of the commodities in a multi-commodity world. We already know how its demand curve is generated. At each price of bread, the prices of other commodities being given, consumers demand the quantity of bread such that the marginal rate of substitution of any other commodity for bread is equal to the ratio of the price of bread to the price of the other commodity. That is to say: if p_b is the price of bread, if MRS is the number of units of some commodity X that a typical consumer is just willing to have substituted for a loaf of bread, and if p_x is the price of commodity X, then at price p_b consumers will demand the amount of bread such that $p_b = \text{MRS} \cdot p_x$.

The supply curve reflects a similar balancing of alternatives on the part of producers. At any price of bread, the prices of other commodities (including factors of production) being given, producers will supply the quantity of bread for which the marginal cost is equal to that price. But factors of production will be priced so that the marginal cost is the opportunity cost—i.e., the value of the other commodities that could be made with the resources required to produce a loaf of bread. That is to say: if p_b is the price of a loaf, if MRT is the number of units of commodity X that can be made by the resources used in producing a loaf, and if p_x is the price of commodity X, then the quantity of bread that will be supplied at price p_b will satisfy $p_b = \text{MRT} \cdot p_x$.

If the price clears the market for bread, so that the quantities demanded and supplied are equal, both of these equalities hold, so that in comparison with any other commodity

$$MRS(X \text{ for bread}) = \frac{p_b}{p_x} = MRT(X \text{ for bread}).$$

This equation asserts that when markets are in equilibrium, a typical consumer's marginal rate of substitution of any commodity for bread will be equal to the economy's marginal rate of transformation of that commodity for bread. More generally, when all markets are in equilibrium, the consumers' marginal rate of substitution between any pair of commodities will be equal to the marginal rate of transformation between them according to the production possibility frontier. When this happens, the bundle of commodities that is being produced is the one that accords with consumers' sovereignty, for this is the consumer sovereignty condition. (A long way back, in Chapter 2, we saw that competitive markets with freely adjusting prices operate to bring about this result.)

The big world is not so very different, after all, from Robinson Crusoe. When market-clearing prices are established for all commodities, each consumer is confronted, in effect, with a miniature version of the allocative choices faced by the whole economy. The consumer has to decide how much to buy of each commodity, and in making this decision the terms on which he can have more of one commodity in exchange for taking less of another (the ratio of their prices) are identical with the terms on which the economy as a whole can produce more of one commodity at the cost of producing less of some other (their marginal rates of transformation). Therefore, the price ratios tell the consumer the economic cost of every commodity he buys, in terms of the commodities that must be foregone in order to produce it, and by the same token the consumer, in making his choices, tells the producers how much of other commodities he is willing to forego in order to obtain the ones he buys.

Thus the familiar demand and supply curves are the instruments by which a populous economy brings together the facts of life about its production possibilities and the desires of its consumers. No one in a real economy knows its production possibility frontier, still less the indifference maps of its consumers. No matter. The supply and demand curves convey the information implicitly and guide the economy, by millions of decentralized decisions, to the most appropriate point on its production possibility frontier.

REVIEW OF THE PRICE MECHANISM

In Chapter 7 we established that an efficiently running economy should do three things: (1) it should distribute its output among consumers in such a way that no consumers could benefit from a reallocation that did not harm any others; (2) it should produce as much of every commodity as possible without reducing the output of any other commodity; and (3) it should produce a bundle of commodities such that no other producible bundle is preferred by every consumer. We noticed that these are very modest requirements in a way; they are the least common denominator of what every member of the economy can be expected to agree on. But from another point of view they are a very tall order. They require an extraordinary degree of coordination of economic activity and of responsiveness to consumers' desires. They require vast quantities of information to be transmitted from consumers to producers and back.

Nevertheless, an economy organized on the basis of freely responding competitive markets will meet all three requirements without imposing the straitjacket of centralized planning or direction.

1. It achieves efficient distribution by charging all consumers the same prices. These prices induce each consumer to proportion his purchases among commodities so that his marginal rate of substitution between every pair of commodities is the same as that of every other consumer, and this is the condition for efficient distribution.

2. It achieves efficient production by charging all firms the same prices for the productive factors they use. The profit motive then insures that each firm will produce the most valuable outputs it can with the productive factors it uses, and that no factor will be used in a firm if some other firm can employ it to produce an output that consumers value more highly. The result is an output bundle on the production possibility frontier.

3. It enforces consumer sovereignty by permitting prices to vary until the quantities supplied and demanded are equated for all commodities. Price variations can achieve this unless there is macroeconomic disequilibrium (that is, unless some consumers desire to hoard some of their incomes in the form of money). When the supplies and demands of all commodities are in balance, consumers are as well satisfied as is physically and technically possible, because then each consumer's **135** marginal rate of substitution between every pair of commodities is equal to the

marginal rate of transformation between them. When this equality holds, no transfer of resources is possible between any pair of commodities that will increase the supply of one of them more than just enough to compensate consumers for the reduction in the supply of the other.

These feats establish the price system as a remarkably subtle and ingenious social contrivance. The price system has its limitations, which we shall discuss in the next few sections, but the fundamental fact to remember is its power to elicit and transmit essential economic information and to stimulate appropriate decisions by producers and consumers.

THE DISTRIBUTION OF INCOME

We have placed adequate emphasis on the importance of our three criteria of economic efficiency, and also on their limitations. Their most severe limitation is that they are devoid of ethical, moral, and aesthetic content—a limitation particularly damaging in matters concerning the distribution of wealth and income in any economy. Economic principles, being unanimity principles, do not provide any guidance for the distribution of income, an issue which is charged inherently with conflict of interest. Yet the distribution of income is very likely the most important question in economics, and one of the most important issues confronting any society. (A hundred and fifty years ago, Ricardo wrote, "To determine the laws which regulate this distribution is the principal problem in Political Economy.") It towers over any of the fine points of resource allocation that we have discussed; and, in fact, the whole theory of allocation was developed as a byproduct of the search for the laws of income distribution, much as chemistry emerged as a byproduct of the search for the philosopher's stone.

Though economics has nothing to teach about how income should be distributed, it has a great deal to say about how income is distributed in an economy with free markets. In such an economy, income is distributed as an incidental result of producing goods and services. Each participant receives the market value of the resources under his control that he devotes to economic effort, usually his own labor. The market values of productive resources are determined by supply and demand in the same way as the prices of any other commodities. The distribution of income in a market economy, then, depends on two things. One is the distribution of control over factors of production; i.e., the distribution of wealth. This is largely an historical and sociological matter. The other is the prices of the different productive resources. These prices, in turn, depend on the supply and demand curves of the resources.

Demand curves have been discussed before—principally in Chapter 4, where we found that the quantity of any factor demanded at any price is the quantity for which the value of the marginal product of the factor (the same in all firms that employ it) is equal to that price. We emphasized that the demand curve alone does not determine the price or wage or rent of the factor. For complete determination, of course, the supply curve is needed, too. The supply curve of a factor of production depends upon the nature of that factor. It has been usual since the time of Adam Smith, at least, to divide all factors of production into three great classes, *labor, land,* and *capital.* They have to be discussed individually.

The Wages of Labor

Labor includes all factors of production whose application is inseparable from the person of the supplier. Supplying labor is therefore not an ordinary act of purchase-and-sale; taking a job amounts to choosing a way of life. From this it can be inferred, correctly, that the supply of labor is not very responsive to changes in wage rates. This is true, both as regards the total amount of labor supplied by a population, and as regards the supply of labor of specific types in specific places. Men do not lightly change their employment in response to wage changes. The size of the total labor force is even less responsive, since the core of the labor force is the population of able-bodied men, all of whom normally work in our society.

The supply of labor is not completely unresponsive to wage changes, however. The amount of labor offered grows when wages are exceptionally high: young people go to work sooner, old people retire later, employed men work overtime and "moonlight," housewives accept part-time and full-time jobs. In addition, the supplies of specific sorts of labor respond to wage changes, especially in the long run: students train themselves for specialties that they expect to be well-paid; migration to California is sensitive to wage and employment conditions there. But, in spite of these and other modes of response, labor is a particularly viscous commodity that flows only sluggishly to where it is needed.

To the normal sociological resistances that impede movement from one job to another we must add a number of artificial impediments. In many occupations, trade unions and professional associations keep a careful control over the supply of accredited labor in the interest of assuring ample employment to their members. This is true of a wide range of workers, including actuaries, bakers, carpenters, druggists, and electricians (but not economists, a selfless lot).

The supply curve for any type of labor arises from considerations such as these; the demand curve for each type of labor follows directly from its marginal productivity. The intersection of the two curves determines the wage and the level of employment of that type of labor. Each worker is paid according to the marginal productivity of his type of skill, but what that productivity is depends on labor supply as well as on demand conditions. The greater the supply of any type of labor in general, the lower will be its marginal productivity.

The Rent of Land

Ricardo defined land to be "the original and indestructible powers of the soil." Nowadays, economists prefer to conceive of land more abstractly as comprising all factors of production that cannot be created or destroyed. (By this definition, even a television channel is a kind of land.) It follows from the definition that the supply of any kind of land is totally inelastic; it is simply there, and is available for use or hire no matter what the rent is. The forces of competition determine the rent of land to be its marginal productivity when the given supply is fully employed, and if a particular kind of land is in plentiful supply, its rent may fall to zero.

Capital consists of all produced means of production separable from human persons. Since capital can be produced, it has a sloping supply curve which plays a part in determining the rate of hire of capital, called the *interest rate*.

The determination of the rate of interest is one of the more confusing aspects of economics, and we shall not delve deeply into it. The confusion results partly from the fact that capital is not a measurable entity, but is a collection of diverse objects called *capital goods*. Each machine, tractor, office building, article in inventory, or any other thing that assists in the work of the economy, is a capital good. But each is also an ordinary commodity whose price is determined by principles already explained.

The supply curve of a capital good is the marginal-cost curve of the industry that produces it. The demand curve depends on its marginal productivity, the amount that the annual profits of a firm would increase if it were acquired. Here is where the complication arises: the price of a capital good cannot be compared directly with its marginal productivity because a capital good is likely to last a long time. For example, a truck costing $5,000 might be expected to save a firm $1,400 a year. Would the truck be worth acquiring (i.e., would the truck be demanded) at that price? The answer is not apparent from the two figures given. It depends on the life of the truck (7 years, let us assume) and on how much $5,000 can earn when invested in other ways.

A little compound-interest figuring will show that a loan of $5,000 repayable in 7 annual installments of $1,400 each earns an interest rate of 20 per cent per year. If the firm can borrow for less than 20 per cent interest, it would be wise to do so and buy the truck. This, of course, is true in general. Whatever the rate of interest may be, firms will be willing to borrow or to use their own funds to acquire all capital goods that can earn more than the going rate of interest.

From this, several things follow. The earning prospects of every capital good can be expressed as a rate of return on its price, just as we have done with the truck. Firms will acquire capital goods to the point where the rate of return on one more unit (the marginal rate of return) will be approximately the same for every type of capital goods, and for all will be about equal to the rate of interest at which firms can borrow. The market rate of interest therefore determines the total amount of money that firms would like to invest: the lower the rate of interest, the greater the amount of investment that will appear profitable. We can call the relationship between the rate of interest and the amount that firms would like to invest in capital goods the *demand curve for capital*.[5]

The *supply curve for capital* shows correspondingly the amount that would be available for investment in capital goods in relationship to the market rate of interest. The rate of interest serves to entice funds into investment uses. When it is low, people prefer to keep their wealth in the form of ready cash and to use their incomes for consumption. For these reasons, less money is available for investment at low rates of interest than at high ones. The supply curve for capital slopes upward like the supply curve for an ordinary commodity.

The intersection of these two curves determines the market rate of interest, the total amount of investment or demand for capital goods, and the rate of return

[5] In this context, the word "capital" is used to mean the dollar value of funds to be invested in capital goods.

earned by the marginal unit of every kind of capital good. It determines, therefore, the income earned per dollar by owners of capital.[6]

PERSONAL INCOME DISTRIBUTION

The price of a unit of the services of every factor of production is determined by the principles just given. The principle of marginal productivity is at work in every case: each factor commands a return equal to the value of its marginal product in the application where it is most valuable. In this way a free market economy achieves the most productive use of its resources but, at the same time, a rather callous distribution of income among its members.

Each individual's income depends upon the amounts and types of resources that he owns. Texas oilmen, renowned surgeons, Ringo Starr, and other possessors of highly productive resources receive enormous incomes. The rest of us receive less, sometimes pitifully little. Typical results are shown in Table 8-1. Only six per cent of American families received an income of over $15,000 in 1964, yet disposed of more than a quarter of the total consumers' income. At the other end of the scale, a sixth of the families had an income of less than $3,000 but shared about only one-twentieth of the total income of consumers.

If there is any ethical standard implicit in this system of income distribution, it is that deservingness consists in ability and willingness to contribute to economic output. Even if it be conceded that some incentives are needed to stimulate men to the efforts that society desires most, there is no assurance that the incentives provided by unfeeling markets are of just the right strength. In fact, the general social opinion seems to be that the automatic incentives are too strong, and we take steps to moderate them. Progressive income taxes reduce the earnings of

---

[6] For a more complete discussion of the determination and consequences of the rate of interest see Charles L. Schultze, *National Income Analysis*, 2nd ed., in this Series.

Table 8-1   DISTRIBUTION OF INCOME AMONG FAMILIES,
UNITED STATES, 1964

Income	Percentage of Families	Percentage of Total Income Received by Families
Less than $1,000	3	*
$1,000-$1,999	7	2
$2,000-$2,999	8	3
$3,000-$3,999	9	4
$4,000-$4,999	9	4
$5,000-$5,999	10	7
$6,000-$6,999	10	8
$7,000-$9,999	23	23
$10,000-$14,999	16	23
$15,000 and over	6	26

* Less than ½%.

139

Source: *Statistical Abstract of the United States, 1966*, pp. 335, 336. Some data interpolated.

exceptional talents and fortunate ownership. Social security legislation and minimum wage laws set a floor below incomes, and bankruptcy laws soften the penalties of poor business judgment. We are perpetually seeking compromises between a system of income distribution that stimulates men to put forth their best efforts, and one that conforms to generally held concepts of social justice.

THE LIMITS OF THE PRICE SYSTEM

Before concluding, we have to consider a different sort of question: If the price system is as sensitive, responsive, potent, and efficient as we have portrayed it to be, why doesn't society entrust all social decisions to it; why do we need any other social institutions at all? This question is not intended to raise any serious doubts about the need for governments and all their works. It is intended, rather, to help us look more closely at the distinguishing characteristics of decisions made in the marketplace, to see what they can and cannot be expected to accomplish. By examining the reasons for the traditional roles of business and government, we shall gain some insight into the proper location of the boundary between them, a boundary which has been in dispute since the cry of *laissez faire* was first raised in the eighteenth century.

The main virtue we have claimed for leaving certain social decisions to private firms and markets is that, under proper conditions, decisions so made will be productively efficient and responsive to individual consumers' preferences. Accordingly, we rely on the market for decisions when both of two conditions are met: when it appears that the market will respond efficiently to consumers' desires, and when it is socially desirable to honor individual preferences. These conditions are violated in many important instances, some of which we now examine.

Decreasing Long-Run Costs

We have already discussed one of the most important circumstances in which competitive markets cannot function: industries in which there are strongly increasing returns to scale. In such industries, competition breaks down into either oligopoly or monopoly. Oligopolistic industries, in spite of their sluggishness, behave tolerably like competitive ones so long as the oligopolists do not collude with each other. The government inhibits collusion through its antitrust policy and relies on oligopolistic industries, under mild supervision, to approximate competitive behavior.

The regulation of industries in which monopoly cannot be prevented is much more stern. Either the industry is declared a public utility and regulated very closely, or else, as in the case of water supply, the government provides the commodity itself.

Competence of Consumers

We have assumed implicitly, especially in Chapter 5, that when a consumer divides his budget among commodities with the intent of equating the marginal rate of substitution between each pair to the ratio of their prices, he has a good chance of succeeding. Otherwise, if the consumer has no basis for judging the satisfaction that a commodity will give him, or if he is easily misled, then he cannot be expected to attain the highest indifference curve that his budget permits, and no claim can be made for the efficiency of relying on consumers' choices.

Indeed, there is likely to be a positive inducement to mislead consumers when they are unable to appraise the quality or serviceability of commodities offered.

Substantial economic waste can result if the markets for such commodities are allowed to operate without impediment, and society is likely to intervene in those markets either by requiring disclosure of information or by substituting the appraisal of competent judges for that of individual consumers. Anyone who wishes to practice law or medicine must be licensed by some expert board. The government audits the books of banks and insurance companies, as individual customers cannot. The Federal Trade Commission detects and prohibits false or misleading advertising and packaging. The Food and Drug Administration and local health departments supervise the cleanliness and safety of food, drugs, and restaurants. These are but examples of the many ways in which the government intervenes in markets to create conditions in which they can respond to relatively well-informed expressions of consumers' preferences, rather than to misjudgments.

Public Goods

The essential functions of government arise from circumstances in which there is no way for an individual consumer to express his preferences through ordinary market channels. It helps to think of these circumstances as divided into two types, though most actual cases are blends between them. One type is concerned with the provision of *public goods,* which are goods that cannot be left to individual initiative for social reasons. Police protection and law courts are leading examples of one class of public goods; it would be socially destructive to permit individuals to provide these goods for themselves or through private arrangements. They must, for the harmony of society, be provided socially and equitably.

The other major class of public goods comprises those that cannot be provided to any individual without being provided simultaneously to many others whether they want them or not. Leading instances are national defense, public health services, and flood protection. With respect to them we are all, perforce, in the same boat; no individual can decide for himself how much he will receive of any of them because he must receive the same amount as everybody else. Ordinary markets cannot tell how much of such a good, or of what kind, should be provided, and such decisions are made universally by other means.

External Effects

The other type of circumstance in which markets cannot give effect to individual preferences arises when one individual's choice has beneficial or untoward effects on other individuals who have no voice in the decision. Such effects are often called *external effects,* neighborhood effects, or spill-overs, and are very prevalent.

Education is one of the most important examples of a beneficial spill-over. In the early nineteenth century, when education was still a matter for individual choice, illiteracy was widespread among the poorer levels of the population. This was recognized as a social evil, inconsistent with democratic government and with the cultivation of the human mind and spirit. In other words, it was recognized that Mr. A had a legitimate interest in the extent to which Mr. B educated his children. But Mr. B did not take account of outsiders' interests when he allocated

141

his budget. He decided on the amount of education for his children (e.g., eldest son only, first four grades) by the usual principle of equating its marginal rate of substitution for other commodities to its price or opportunity cost to him.

The price system led to a correct level of education, in comparison with the other forms of expenditure, from Mr. B's point of view, but not from the point of view of society—that is, not from the point of view of Mr. A and many others who felt so strongly about it that they were willing to contribute to the cost of educating B's children. Their welfare could be promoted, without harm to Mr. B, by permitting them to contribute to the cost of education, but ordinary markets do not permit this. Free public education fills this need: [7] it permits realization of the external benefits of education. In the same way, by subsidizing public housing and beneficial forms of recreation (through parks, libraries, museums), external benefits are reaped as a byproduct of individual consumption which would be lost if the full cost were charged to the direct consumer. Such nonmarket devices can make an economy more responsive to consumer sovereignty than can undeviating reliance on the price system.

In the case of education, private benefits are less than social benefits in the sense that third parties are willing to contribute to promote the consumption of the commodity. The divergence between private and social benefits may run in the other direction: sometimes we should be willing to pay other individuals to desist from actions that diminish our well-being, and they would be willing to accept. There is a loss of over-all welfare if, as is usually the case, there is no market for carrying out the transaction.

There are all-too-many examples of this situation. One of the most pressing at present is the increasing pollution of our streams and other waters. Clean water is a scarce good, yet we often behave as though its use had nothing to do with economics. Factories and cities dump their waste into nearby streams because it is cheaper for them to do so than to purify their outflows or to carry their wastes out to sea. But this practice is likely to impose costs on users farther down the stream. In effect, clean water is inefficiently allocated: upstream users have unlimited supplies, while downstream users are frequently deprived. It is not used where its marginal productivity is highest.

To put our fingers on exactly where this economic waste arises, let us think of a river with a papermill, dye works, or other heavy polluter far upstream. Under current arrangements, this plant dumps waste into the river virtually without restriction. But every ton of waste imposes costs on downstream users. Suppose it costs them 50¢ per ton of waste to treat the water, obtain clean water from more expensive sources, or otherwise overcome the effects of the pollution. Then some of the cost of producing paper, let us say, has been transferred to other sectors of the economy. The marginal cost of paper, which includes only the value of commodities traded on markets, will be less than the true value of the resources required to produce it, one of which is the clean water that the mill destroys. Accordingly, the mill owners will ignore this element of cost and will produce more paper at the site and will use water more lavishly than is consistent with attaining the production possibility frontier. If the mill were charged 50¢ per ton of waste discharged into the stream, the situation would be corrected. But there is no market to impose this charge. It could be done by government decree, if the appropriate amount to

[7] Compulsory public education goes even further: it provides the external benefits even at the cost of diminishing the welfare of the consumers directly involved.

charge were known (and this has been proposed as a national policy), but the correct charge is exceedingly difficult to determine without the aid of a market.

Air pollution, traffic congestion, and noise generation are all similar to water pollution in that ordinary market processes fail to make visible to deciders the full costs to society of certain activities. Sometimes we tolerate the resultant waste of resources, sometimes we try to reduce it by imposing government controls. But government regulation is crude and insensitive by comparison with market processes. How can we tell, for example, whether the noise reduction achieved by requiring aircraft to fly 1,000 feet higher than they do is worth the additional costs and hazards of steeper ascents from airports?

Some Other Complications

Throughout, we have ignored two very important characteristics of economic life. One is *the process of adjustment to market conditions.* The efficiency characteristics of a price system are valid when all markets are in equilibrium, but they never are. And so the possibility arises that the processes of attaining equilibrium may be so slow and costly that the benefits are never reaped, and substantial resources are wasted in ineffectual attempts to attain equilibrium. There are surely many ill-conceived investment projects in any economy, resulting from businessmen's efforts to meet market demands that exist only temporarily, during the process of adjustment. For example, an increase in the demand for aluminum which cannot be satisfied in the short run may so increase the demand for copper and its price that new copper smelters are mistakenly installed. Businessmen try to avoid this kind of error by using other sources of information than current prices—in particular, trade and business news, and market forecasting techniques. The government assists by providing invaluable financial and business data. Still, the process of finding equilibrium is an intricate and slow one. It is, indeed, the businessman's primary social function, for it appears that no one can judge the complexities of an industry better than the men who are intimately engaged in it.

The other central characteristic we have ignored thus far is *uncertainty in economic life,* the fact that no one can be sure what the results of a business decision will be. Uncertainty would be substantially reduced in a static economy in full equilibrium, so this problem is closely related to the preceding one. But even in equilibrium, businessmen would not know the marginal productivities of many of the factors they employ, or the shapes of the demand curves for their products, or many of the other complicated data that we have assumed known in our discussions.

In fact, then, a businessman can hardly be expected to equate a marginal productivity he does not know to a marginal revenue he can only guess at. Our analysis of business decisions, therefore, has to be interpreted as largely schematic, and the results we obtained as approximations. More advanced treatments that allow for the inherent vagueness of business information lead to basically the same conclusions.

For these last two reasons, the price and market system hardly ever works as advertised, and because of the difficulties discussed previously, it fails to work at all in many important cases. We are constantly faced with the need to tamper with it, and occasionally to supersede it entirely in some respects. Yet even when market performance is falling short of the ideal, we should keep in mind that the governmental controls that we can impose lack the responsiveness to consumers' wishes, and the power to elicit efficient performance that competitive market processes possess. In disputed cases (and there are many), the presumption should be in favor of leaving economic guidance to free markets. Only they permit consumers to express their preferences effectively, and only they preserve the diffusion of economic power that, experience confirms, is one of the necessary attributes of a free society.

SUMMARY

An economic system is a set of social institutions for organizing and guiding the work of providing goods and services in a community. Three criteria that a perfectly efficient economy would satisfy and that an actual one should approximate are as follows:

1. Efficient distribution of commodities. This condition is satisfied when all consumers share the same marginal rate of substitution between every pair of commodities, for then no exchange of commodities among consumers could benefit any consumer without harming some others.

2. Efficient production of commodities. This condition requires that the value of the marginal product of every resource be the same in every industry and firm that employs it, for then no reallocation of resources among firms could increase the total value of the economy's output or could increase the output of any commodity without reducing the output of some other. Symbolically, we write that if factor X is used to produce commodities A and B, then

$$p_A \text{MP}(X \text{ used for } A) = p_B \text{MP}(X \text{ used for } B)$$

where p_A, p_B are the prices of the two commodities and $\text{MP}(X \text{ used for } A)$, $\text{MP}(X \text{ used for } B)$ are the marginal products of X when used to produce the two commodities.

3. Consumer sovereignty, or producing the commodities that consumers want to the greatest extent possible. This condition holds when the marginal rate of transformation between every pair of commodities equals the ratio of their prices, which in turn equals the marginal rate of substitution between them, common to all consumers. Symbolically:

$$\text{MRT}(A \text{ for } B) = \frac{p_B}{p_A} = \text{MRS}(A \text{ for } B).$$

These three criteria of economic efficiency and their implications apply to nonmonetary as well as to price economies, as our study of a simple two-commodity example showed. They are weak criteria, however, and may lead to results inconsistent with a community's standards of social justice.

The combinations of goods and services among which an economy must choose are described by its production possibility frontier, which shows the greatest amount of each commodity that can be produced in conjunction with specified quantities of every other commodity. It is wasteful for an economy to produce an output that is not on its frontier, and the frontier can always be reached by following the principle of comparative advantage. This principle holds that when there is a choice among the factors to be used to produce any commodity, that factor should be chosen whose productivity when used for that commodity is greatest in proportion to its productivity in alternative employments. Firms that trade in competitive markets obey this principle automatically.

The marginal rate of transformation between two commodities is the number of units of one that have to be sacrificed if sufficient resources are transferred to increase the output of the other by one unit. This concept enables us to specify the point on the production possibility frontier at which consumers' sovereignty is obeyed, as was done above in summarizing the third criterion of economic efficiency. The location of this point depends on the shape of the production possibility frontier, the indifference curves of individual consumers, and the distribution of income among consumers.

The relevance of the distribution of income can be seen from the box diagram for the allocation among consumers of the output corresponding to a point on the production possibility frontier. Efficient distribution requires that the allocation correspond to one of the points on the contract curve in the box diagram, since that curve contains all points where the consumers have a common marginal rate of substitution. Each point on the contract curve represents a different distribution of income, and the common marginal rate of substitution is likely to be different at the different points.

Each point on the production possibility frontier not only represents a different output of commodities, but corresponds to different marginal rates of transformation between commodities, and therefore to a different set of prices. Since the distribution of income changes when prices change, following the dictates of consumers' sovereignty can be intricate; two data are changing at the same time. There is, however, a point on the frontier with the essential property that if prices corresponding to the marginal rates of transformation there are charged, then the demand for every commodity will be equal to the supply at that point. At such a point (there may be several) the output, the prices consistent with efficient production, and the distribution of income are all in conformity, and all three criteria of efficiency are satisfied.

In any economy with competitive markets, the price mechanism guides the economy to the consumer sovereignty point on the production possibility frontier. It does this by inducing conformity to two basic formulas. One is

$$\text{MRT}(A \text{ for } B) = \frac{p_B}{p_A} = \text{MRS}(A \text{ for } B)$$

—which was given above. The other is the relation among product prices, factor prices, and marginal productivity. If X is any factor of production used to produce commodity A, if w_x is its wage or rate of hire, and if $\text{MP}(X \text{ used for } A)$ is the marginal product of X when used to produce A, then competition establishes that

$$\text{MP}(X \text{ used for } A) = \frac{w_x}{p_A}.$$

This equation, in conjunction with the preceding one, assures efficiency in production. These two equations are worth remembering since they summarize the gist of the argument for the efficiency of competitive pricing.

The distribution of income in a free market economy is a byproduct of its **145** productive operations; each member receives as income the value of the services of the productive factors he happens to own. The values of these services are determined by the usual principles of supply and demand. The demand curve for any factor results from the fact that the price at which a given quantity will be demanded is the value of its marginal product when that quantity is employed, the same in all industries that use the factor. The supply curves for factors of production arise from other considerations: the amount of labor offered in response to any wage is influenced by sociological and psychological factors, the supply of land is fixed by definition, the supply of capital is determined by the willingness of income receivers to retrench their consumption and to part with ready cash under the inducement of different rates of interest.

Much as the price system can do, it has inherent limitations. It depends on the operation of competitive markets, which tend to break down in the presence of economies of scale. Its responsiveness to consumers' sovereignty makes it vulnerable to consumers' mistakes, which are likely to be serious with respect to certain highly technical or infrequently purchased commodities. By its very nature, it is inapplicable to decisions about public goods—goods concerning which individual consumers cannot make independent consumption decisions. It disregards external effects—the effects of one man's consumption or productive activities on another man's welfare. Its efficiency is substantially reduced in the presence of uncertainty and when markets are not fully in equilibrium. Because of these shortcomings, many important goods and services cannot be provided by private firms operating through markets, and many markets have to be restricted and controlled. Nevertheless, when the conditions required for the effective operation of markets are fairly well fulfilled, markets are the most effective as well as the most democratic mode of economic organization that has yet been developed.

The classic work on the price system is Alfred Marshall, *Principles of Economics*, 8th ed. (London: Macmillan, 1920). It is long and often dull, but full of insight and always understandable. The most famous brief exposition, though somewhat old-fashioned by now, is Sir Hubert Henderson, *Supply and Demand* (Cambridge: Cambridge University Press, 1921 and later).* *The Theory of Price* by George J. Stigler (New York: Macmillan, 1952) is a succinct, intermediate-level treatment of the material covered in this monograph. So is Joe S. Bain, *Price Theory* (New York: Holt, 1952).

Chapters 3 and 4, on the theory of production and the behavior of firms, are influenced by Joel Dean, *Managerial Economics* (Englewood Cliffs, N.J.: Prentice-Hall, 1951). Richard M. Cyert and James J. March, *A Behavioral Theory of the Firm* (Englewood Cliffs, N.J.: Prentice-Hall, 1963) explores the anatomy of decision-making in the firm and contains some instructive case studies. James R. Nelson, ed., *Marginal Cost Pricing in Practice* (Englewood Cliffs, N.J.: Prentice-Hall, 1964) presents some very sophisticated applications of the principles of these chapters. William J. Baumol, *Economic Theory and Operations Analysis,* 2nd ed. (Englewood Cliffs, N.J.: Prentice-Hall, 1965) contains an exposition of maximization within the firm with emphasis on modern techniques, such as linear programming.

For Chapter 5, Ruby Turner Norris, *The Theory of Consumer's Demand* (New Haven: Yale University Press, 1941) is a brief and detailed exposition of the theory of consumption. A modern and rigorous treatment is presented in Peter Newman, *The Theory of Exchange* (Englewood Cliffs, N.J.: Prentice-Hall, 1965). The literary classic on this subject, and very enjoyable, is Thorstein Veblen, *The Theory of the Leisure Class* (New York: Macmillan, 1899, and many other editions).*

The most accessible additional reading about market behavior, Chapter 6, is Richard Caves, *American Industry: Structure, Conduct, Performance,* 2nd ed., in this Series. Two classics in the field are E. A. G. Robinson, *The Structure of Competitive Industry* (Cambridge: Cambridge University Press, 1931) * from an applied point of view, and E. H. Chamberlin, *The Theory of Monopolistic Competition* (Cambridge, Mass.: Harvard University Press, 1933) from a theoretical viewpoint. *The Structure of American Industry,* edited by Walter Adams (New

* Indicates material available in paperback.

York: Macmillan, 1961) * presents a number of interesting case studies. Joe S. Bain, *Industrial Organization* (New York: Wiley, 1959) is a particularly well-informed and thorough text. The best empirical analysis of American industrial structure is probably Bain's *Barriers to New Competition* (Cambridge, Mass.: Harvard University Press, 1956).

There are many important works on the purposes and achievements of the competitive price system. Adam Smith's *Wealth of Nations* (1776 and many later printings) is the greatest statement, but by no means the first. It is still very impressive reading. Most of the concepts discussed in Chapters 7 and 8 are covered in Baumol's *Economic Theory and Operations Analysis,* cited above. Some of the interesting conceptual issues are analyzed in Lionel Robbins, *An Essay on the Nature and Significance of Economic Science,* 2nd ed. (London: Macmillan, 1935) and the entire theory is expounded beautifully in Tjalling C. Koopmans, *Three Essays on the State of Economic Science* (New York: McGraw-Hill, 1957). Koopman's presentation is mathematical in spirit, but accessible. E. H. Phelps Brown, *The Framework of the Pricing System* (London: Chapman and Hall, 1936) presents the whole theory of price with emphasis on the general equilibrium system.

The towering classic on welfare economics is A. C. Pigou, *The Economics of Welfare* (London: Macmillan, 1920). Reading it is a formidable task, but there is no real substitute. The best text is probably Tibor Scitovsky, *Welfare and Competition* (Chicago: Irwin, 1951). Abba P. Lerner, *The Economics of Control* (New York: Macmillan, 1946) is a more modern and terser treatment of the same theory. Charles J. Hitch and Roland N. McKean, *The Economics of Defense in the Nuclear Age* (Cambridge, Mass.: Harvard University Press, 1960) is a fascinating application of the principles of economic allocation. Friedrich A. von Hayek (ed.), *Collectivist Economic Planning* (London: Routledge, 1935) contains thoughtful, though hostile, assessments of the possibilities of applying those principles in a socialist state.